Desperately Seeking Susans

D1737851

Desperately Seeking Susans

edited by
Sarah Yi-Mei Tsiang

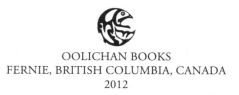

OOLICHAN BOOKS
FERNIE, BRITISH COLUMBIA, CANADA
2012

Library and Archives Canada Cataloguing in Publication

Desperately seeking Susans / Sarah Yi-Mei Tsiang.

ISBN 978-0-88982-287-0

    1. Canadian poetry (English)--Women authors. 2. Canadian

poetry (English)--21st century. I. Tsiang, Yi-Mei, 1978-

PS8283.W6D48 2012   C811'.60809287   C2012-905363-5

We gratefully acknowledge the financial support of the Canada Council for the Arts, the British Columbia Arts Council through the BC Ministry of Tourism, Culture, and the Arts, and the Government of Canada through the Book Publishing Industry Development Program, for our publishing activities.

Published by
Oolichan Books
P.O. Box 2278
Fernie, British Columbia
Canada V0B 1M0

www.oolichan.com

SUSAN

She loved the name so much,
that's what she called her
male bull dog, her rubber boots,
her yellow bike. She even
named her toothbrush
so every day Susan
would be the first thing
and the last
her mouth would know.

—Lorna Crozier

ی

For you, Susan

INTRODUCTION

I am a loud reader. I can't help but snort, cry, and giggle my way through books. My ever-patient husband can tell you that I also have a tendency to follow people around reading poetry to them whether they like it or not. My husband has heard hundreds of read-aloud poems this way, as he gets the mail, makes dinner, or tries to go the bathroom in peace. This is how I first discovered the beauty that is Susan-based poetry. Sitting on the couch one day, I idly said to my husband "I'm thinking of a Canadian poet named Susan, who I love. Guess who?" After he named seven Susans (none of which were the particular Susan I was thinking of) we were both too filled with laughter to continue.

And so this anthology was born, a celebration of the ridiculous surfeit of talent we can easily find in not only Canadian poets, and not only in female Canadian poets, but in female Canadian poets named Susan. All of the poets featured in *Desperately Seeking Susans* have been chosen for the beauty of her work; the coincidence of their names is just the pimento in the olive.

This unapologetically whimsical anthology is more than just a premise: the Susans featured in *Desperately Seeking Susans* have won just about every major literary award there is to win in Canada. When we sent out a call for submissions, we were overwhelmed by the deluge of Susans who had been writing (some in secret, some for the first time). My seven Susans expanded into an anthology featuring 40 Susans, and unfortunately, we had to turn down a huge amount of Susans simply because of space limitation. Within the anthology the poems display a vast range of style and subject matter. When I was first thinking of ordering the book into themes, I was stymied. Where do you put the origin tale of the litchi? Or the poem that introduced me to the term "crotch rocket?" In the end, this book is arranged like a wild garden; there is wanton beauty wherever you turn.

My tendency to read aloud has made itself into a book. These are the poems that have sustained me, that have taught me, and that have haunted me. It is a joy to present to you these, my favourite Susans.

Sarah Yi-Mei Tsiang
Editor

CONTENTS

SUSAN

SUE

SUZIE

SUZANNE

Sue Goytill.

susan Glickman

Susan Elmslie

Susan Holbrook

Susan Musgrave

Sue Sinclair

SUSAN

SUSAN ELMSLIE

FIRST APOLOGY TO MY DAUGHTER

I birthed you like an animal,
soft flanks rising with calm
deepening breaths, brown eyes indifferent
to the hands of well-meaning helpers.
After hours of baffled pushing
and an enfilade of sutures, I surrendered
you to the nursery, just
a couple of hours,
while my body sunk into the mattress
like a slug sinks back into the earth
after its encounter with a shovel.
I didn't know the harried nurse
would think it best not to wake me
to feed you. You yearning
for your first milk
while I dozed
on some far off platform.
That you would tighten
the coil of your body trying to burst
the seam of your swaddling blanket, and cry
that tremulous muscular cry
and me out of earshot. Cry
long enough to give up on crying.
What darkness then, in the fluorescent hours
of the maternity ward while
I taught you the ferocity of hunger.

SUE MACLEOD

NO ONE LIKE US

She was walking along her new street one night in what her agent called
a recently discovered kind of neighbourhood, going to the store where
they sell cigarettes one at a time & know everyone's name & brand,
when she noticed a light in a window upstairs, the curtain was open, the
wall was a turquoise *too* turquoise a colour like the very orange powder
that comes in Kraft Dinner, the pink of cotton candy or something else
with too much sugar or too much whatever, mascara, or Jesus, she was
thinking how it only takes a patch of colour on a wall like that to tell
her this building hasn't been done yet, no one like us lives here

& thinking of her two small sons how they wouldn't know that yet, they
wouldn't know it from seeing the man who came into view, she could
tell he'd been handsome once & still had a certain charm, sinewy arm
raised, a gesture to someone just out of her range, like the pack of
Export A's, the Olands she imagined on the table—a man who might
give them some money for candy, who'd dig in his pocket, liking their
smiles & not thinking at all of their teeth, she was thinking

not without nostalgia of the ache in country music, of neighbours on
the front porch on a summer night & thinking of her two small sons &
things she didn't know at their age: certain scientific facts like the
reason for rainbows & how we divide & divide in our cells.

SUSAN GLICKMAN

POEM ABOUT YOUR LAUGH

When you laugh it is all the unsynchronized clocks
in the watchmaker's shop
striking their dissident hours.
It is six blind kittens having the nipples plucked
from their mouths.
It is the ecstatic susurrus of prayer wheels.

When you laugh innumerable
pine trees shed their needles at once on one side
of the forest, indefinably altering the ecosystem.
A thousand miles away
two sharks lose their taste for blood,
mate, start a new species.

When you laugh your mouth
is the Mammoth Cave in Kentucky
and I can curl up there among the bats
intercepting their sonar.
Oh, your mouth is a diver's bell;
it takes me down untold fathoms.

And when you laugh, old dogs limp
to new patches of sunlight
which they bury for later, knowing something
about need.

SUSAN MUSGRAVE

THE CORONER AT THE TAVERNA

sees everyone's future; it's his
business. He sees the one
with the beautiful neck that will
soon be broken by the other
with the sensitive hands sitting
next to her, sipping a Corona.
He sees the one who will come to him
in pieces, her body dismembered
by an estranged lover because,
as he confessed to the press,
she wouldn't give him any. The coroner
will be careful to note
the body has not been interfered with.

At night he comes to the taverna
to be alone, the sickness he has tasted
during the day consuming his thoughts
like beauty. And beauty is what he seeks
though how you know beauty when you see it
is the question he asks each time he cuts
open a young body and finds something
beautiful but malignant inside. There are
things he won't discuss with anyone,
even the boys who bring him illicit
pleasures, boys he can be
himself with again, when the knife's rinsed.

In the taverna he does not have to think
what will become of these boys once beauty
has outgrown them and they have turned

into uncertain men. He does not have to see
the one who lies before him on the slab,
a long way from home and the pleasures
they shared, the drugs, the cigarettes, his
grotesque lungs now squeezing upwards
into his collarbones, to suck their last
small breath. At the taverna
he does not have to see the track marks
on the boy's skinny arm sticking out
from under him on the bed. The coroner
can sometimes forget the boy's grace, the way
he kneeled to kiss those forbidden places: nothing
touches him here, not even love.

ALONE

You stuck one of Ryan's glow-in-the-dark stars
on the closet door. It's been so dark and the star

holds the memory of light, is part of the constellation
of *us*, of *before*, of *remember*. One of the last

stars to appear in our sky. I tuck Robyn in, wait at her door
for her second I love you, call Ryan up from downstairs

then turn out the lights. It's been so dark and now darker.
I lie in bed and think: the cat's out, the wind and the window

are at it again. The ceiling is its own universe, a blank expanse
of sleeplessness. And the star, a guide to the small light

of my loneliness: your closed closet door, the expanse of ceiling
mirrored in the ocean of empty bed. This the darkest voyage,

the ocean swelling, the star so small, every bone of me
awake, hulled, desperate for land.

෴

It's not that I forget
the cat outside. She just wants to stay out
all night. And it's her cry,
plaintive and despairing: *forgotten, forgotten*
each morning that wakes me.
And each morning, I open the door
to her joy at finally being remembered.

This is her nature, the nightly melodrama
and relief of morning. If dogs look like
their owners, basset hounded,
beagled, then cats are our hearts:
the purring, the nine lives. The mornings
despairing, plaintive: *forgotten, forgotten.*

Can't we both be wind, can't we
both be window? O the long nights
of weather, the wedding procession
of rain and glass and the murmured
disbelief from both sides
of the family. Remember
how we laughed when the dog ran into
the patio door to get at the cat
on the other side? If the dog looks like us
and the cat is our heart, what is the glass
but this marriage, the kids' fingerprints
all over it, the blue sky and clouds
of the other side.

⮝

The star is a guide;
the dog resembles.
The cat is always hopeful. It's been
so dark, the bed an ocean,
the ceiling a galaxy
of awake. Darker:

the cat sleeps most of the time;
the dog begs. The bed
cold, each thought a planet
orbiting above it. Darkest:
each planet has its own moons;

each moon its stars. You will stay awake
for many nights charting them
only to finally sleep, wake to the one star
remaining. You will name that star alone,
then get up, let in your heart
but not before it has waited in every corner
of *forgotten*, has seen itself there
on the other side.

SUSAN ELMSLIE

HOW THE LITCHI CAME TO BE

A god found his wife alone with his best archer. Enraged, overtaken
with jealousy, he turned the archer into a stone, smooth as the
archer's draw, dark as the eye of the hart, small as spite. The wife,
crushed by remorse and grief, threw herself down and grasped this
small stone, curling up around it in her white nightdress drenched
with tears. Her lingering desire transformed her: pale flesh wrapped
tightly round a dense dark heart, sweetness of tears. Moved by the
intensity of emotion, the god took pity on the lovers, and tucked
them into a shell-like cocoon where they could embrace for eternity.
The shell warmed and glowed; the lovers' flushed cheeks. This is
how the litchi came to be.

SUSAN HOLBROOK

GOOD EGG BAD SEED

There are people who only cry in private and people who only cry in public.
People who clean their mouse regularly and people who think *Something's
        wrong with my mouse* over and over.
People who recycle, first washing out the cut-off corners of plastic milk sacs
        as solicitously as if they were contact lenses, and people who throw
        Burger King bags out the car window.
People who open the door for you and people you open the door for.
People who open the door for you and you appreciate it and people who
        open the door for you and it's irritating.
People who love it when you open the door for them and people who refuse
        to let you do it, they want to be the door-opener, and you have a little
        fight about it.
People who play Boggle and people who would rather be shot in the head.
People who keep eight rolls of toilet paper in the bathroom at all times and
        people who call out to other people.
You like an epiphany or you like a surprise.
You are a binary thinker or you are and you aren't.
You say you basically dismantle 500 years of Western metaphysics in one
        fell swoop or you nap under a leaf's lip.
You think Modigliani painted nipples too small or you think Emily Carr
        painted trees too big.
You boil too much pasta or you don't boil enough.
You know all the different kinds of lentils or you resent your vegetarian
        dinner guests.
Mangoes aren't worth the hairs in your teeth or they are.
Terror of disorder keeps you up at night or terror of order does.
You have a way with animals or squirrels smell your fear and attack.
You'd like to be cremated because you believe in ethereal reincarnation
        rather than bodily resurrection or you'd like to be cremated just to be

sure you're really dead when they put you down there.
You're not a group person or you go to political rallies and you're the first
　　　to shout 'Shame!' during the speeches.
You go to rallies because you care about the issues or you go to pick up girls.
You eat the dark meat because you prefer it or you eat the dark meat
　　　because other people want the white meat.
You think the only way to respond to a poem is to write another poem or
　　　you think the only way to respond to a poem is to run the other way.
To you, beating the system means making fake passports or beating the
　　　system means breaking the stems off the broccoli in Zehrs.
You once rescued a duck or you once bagged a buck.
Your mother put peanut butter in the gutter of your celery or she filled it
　　　with Cheez Whiz.
You are torn between the Green Party and the NDP or you are torn between
　　　the Alliance and the Christian Heritage Party. Either way, you can say
　　　both are pretty good on the gay issue.
You flex your back or you flick your Bic.
You'd like a cat in a basket or you'd like a bat in a casket.
You think you're too flat in the bazooms or too fat in the caboose.
Are you eyeing up my cup of java or fucking up my vagina?
Howard Hughes ate no oranges and Allen Ginsberg ate them whole,
　　　including rind, pith, and seeds.
You believe in fate and are paralyzed by the thought of your own power-
　　　lessness or you don't believe in fate and are paralyzed by indecision.
You think they don't pick up the phone because they're out of town or you
　　　think they don't pick up because they're screening and they hate you.
You need to smarten up or you need to dumb down.
You are always a bridesmaid never a bride or you are always a bride and
　　　don't have bridesmaids because you pissed off all your friends by marry-
　　　ing their husbands.
People think you are a good egg or a bad seed.
A free spirit or a freeloader.
You subscribe to *Gourmet* magazine or you don't want fruit in soup.
You get Gloria Steinem and Gertrude Stein mixed up or you get the
　　　Bangles and the Go-Go's mixed up.

Or Orson Welles, H.G. Wells and George Orwell.

You see an ad for a Ford SUV claiming their new folding back seat, the result
of sophisticated problem-solving, 'literally lets you have your cake and
eat it too' and you think *literally!?* well, they've just undermined their
argument with an unsophisticated grammatical flaw and you think of
calling the number at the bottom of the page - a little word to the
wise - but of course you would never do such a thing, or you wouldn't
do such a thing except for once when you impulsively called the Real-
Fruit Gummies people to tell them you got a bag with no green
gummies in it, telling yourself they'll want to know about flaws in
production and secretly speculating that they might send you a free bag,
maybe even a crate, maybe a lifetime supply of green ones, but the
eighteen-year-old RealFruit Gummies customer service representative
on the other end just said 'OooooooKay' like you were a complete
nincompoop and now you think *Why not? I've already wasted ten minutes
thinking about this, why not call Ford?* So you call and explain to the
eighteen-year-old kid whose first word is 'OooooooKay' that 'literally'
means not figuratively and that the ad is telling us there's cake in the
truck that we're having and eating, but she's not really cluing in, not
really grasping the urgency of the situation, and at the end of each of
your sentences you hear your own voice in her ears and know that's all
she has to go on, she doesn't know how attractive and sporty and well-
rounded you are and you can tell she is wondering if this is a prank call
or you are a pervert or, worse - as your voice gets both thinner and more
shrill, if that's possible - someone who needs to get out more.

You need to get out more or you need to get in more.

You need to branch out or you need to put down roots.

You think a pap smear involves the Vatican somehow or you have an apron
that says Bar-B-Cutie on it and you wear it.

When you see a flag at half-mast you worry another former prime minis-
ter has died or you worry another Ramone has died.

You prefer the smell of chai, lavender bushes and line-dried laundry or
basketballs, Magic Markers and puddles of gasoline.

You'd rather have to eat too many mini marshmallows or too much kelp.

You've fallen for a line or you've fallen for a sentence.

You are irritable or iterable.

The figurative sway of language being uncommonly effective on you, you
　　　　can't eat blood oranges while you can eat candy-apple red nail polish.
　　　　Or you live in Puce.

Your idea of self-discipline is to abstain from sex or your idea of self-
　　　　discipline is to call yourself a naughty girl and take yourself to bed.

You think Ian Hanomansing was once husky or you think he will be husky.

You think Ian Hanomansing is the next Peter Mansbridge or you think Peter
　　　　Mansbridge is the next Queen Mum.

You'd rather carve a war monument or you'd rather carve a loon.

Artillary or fritillary.

If you could turn back time, you would lock your bike or you would warn
　　　　your students never to open an essay by quoting Cher.

You'd rather be thought of as dumb and actually be smart or you'd rather
　　　　be thought of as smart and actually be dumb.

If you knew you'd be absolutely alone for two months, you'd never get out
　　　　of the bathtub or you'd never get into the bathtub.

You talk loudly in airport lineups or you are Canadian.

You used to think honeycomb was man-made or you used to think Mt.
　　　　Rushmore was a natural phenomenon.

You are in tiptop shape or you are a teapot shape.

You chose or you were born that way.

No pulp or extra pulp.

A breeze blows around you or a breeze blows through you.

You've all but given up on the perennial pursuit for contentment or you're
　　　　content to find a good muffin.

You take the tunnel or you take the bridge.

You pay the toll lady or you play the lotto daily.

You like to watch the sunset or you like to watch the cliché.

You like Bits & Bites or you like Méli-Mélo.

You say 'the island' and mean Vancouver island or you say it and mean P.E.I.

When you get a C you sink into a depression that forever scars your already
　　　　tenuous sense of self-worth or you say 'All right! a C!'

You are a worrywart or you worry about your warts.

V's of geese are disturbing to you when they are asymmetrical, or when they are symmetrical.

If you could have an answer to any question about time, you'd ask whether
time is indeed a Cantorian continuum or if its constitution is granular,
or you would ask why is it still winter.

You jilt or you are jilted.

You tilt or you are tilted.

You think the words 'plethora' and 'penultimate' might as well be used as
long as they're there or you feel it's best to just leave them be, like hotel
shower caps.

Being called a nickname makes you blush and feel pleasantly confused or
you fume when someone calls you Champ, Bud, or H.D. Imagiste.

You feel that as you get older, your horizons expand, or you've been cross-
ing off your options since age eleven, when you had to concede that you
would never be a child chess prodigy, an Olympic gymnast or the
world's shortest veterinarian.

You think Oil of Olay is for your face or you think it's for your tortilla chips.

You think you are more attractive and interesting than you are or you think
you are far more attractive and interesting than you are.

When you knock over a glass you say 'Clumsy me!' or you say 'Who put that
glass there?!' or you say 'Stupid cup'.

You'd rather be knee deep in interoffice memos or knee deep in slugs.

You'd rather have a swan-shaped birthmark on your face or a dimpled knee
that resembles an angry Joe Clark head.

You'd send a picture of it to *Ripley's Believe it or Not* and they would believe
it or not.

You could see yourself in a fake fur thong or you couldn't.

Other people could see you in a fake fur thong or they couldn't.

People could see you in a fake fur thong but wouldn't want to or they
couldn't but would.

Now you want one, don't you? Or don't you.

If you were a figure in a Surrealist painting you'd be propped up or there'd
be a hole through you.

You feel sorry for the mules or you feel sorry for the piano.

Linda McCartney or Heather Mills.

For you, it goes without saying, or it doesn't.

In that one 'you' was really me or 'you' was really you or 'you' was Paul.

And now back to you, you would say, if you were a reporter who forgot
the anchorman's name or if you were playing a very slow game of
Ping-Pong.

Moral DIE-lemma or moral DUH-lemma. Those who say DUH-lemma are
truly having one, whereas those with DIE-lemmas put on a good show
while having decided from the start take the money or sex and run.

Your last words will be 'What is the question' or 'Hey, you're a *jumping*
spider.'

If you had more time you would take a breath at commas, or you would jam
more syllables in, say 'aluminium.'

If you had more time you could be a prolific writer and a long-distance
runner, or an Xbox champion and compulsive masturbator.

You mark the passing of each year with a new piercing or you go to the
jewellers at the mall once, at eighteen, your clammy hand shaking the
jittery paw of the girl who will use the studgun for the first time. She's
been taught to distract you, 'How was your summer?' she asks, punching
a needle into your right lobe. 'Great,' you say and her bracelets clink
against the gun as she centres it over your left lobe. 'How was your
summer?' she asks, *punch*, 'Okay,' you say.

If you could fill a time capsule to inform future generations about our
culture, you would include an article on the loss of the Space Shuttle
Columbia or a tape of *Entertainment Tonight* featuring Ben Affleck's
response to the loss of the Space Shuttle Columbia, since he sat in it once.

You order a bidet for your kitchen because it sounds kind of classy or you
say no to a Bodum because it sounds kind of dirty.

When your women's studies professor says the course will 'not be about
man hating' you feel more comfortable or you are kind of disappointed.

You are a night person or a morning person, that is if 'personhood' is
defined by alertness and productivity. Perhaps 'persons' might ideally be
snoozing on a full stomach in warm slanty sunshine, in a hammock or
perhaps on their desk, cheek pressed to a fluorescent Post-it, in which
case why not be an afternoon person.

Music and poetry are inseparable or music and poetry are in sufferable.

There are two kinds of people, and one of them is Jordan Craddock,

Columbus, Ohio, 1956.
When you borrow a broken pencil from someone, you sharpen in, use it and
          return it sharp so as to effect an even trade, or you sharpen it, use it and
          break it, so as to approximate the condition in which you received it.
That's what Jordan Craddock did.
It was 1956 or '57.
A pregnant lady is a treble clef or a treble clef is a snail on a fork or a snail
          on a fork is something French or something French is anything blue or
          anything blue is anything borrowed or anything borrowed is a burr in
          your boot or a burr in your boot is a tiny dried pufferfish stuck to your
          sock or a tiny dried pufferfish stuck to your sock is always a surprise and
          always a surprise is a pregnant lady, why is that?
Two kinds of people walk into a bar looking for a punchline, find a tedious
          denouement instead.
Smashing through the guardrail and plummeting to your death you shout
          'I love you!' or you should 'Fuck!'
You say 'I love you' or you say 'I love you too.'
You say 'Fuck you' or you say 'Oh yeah? Fuck you.'
And in the end the love you took is equal to the love you mook.
The medium is the message, or raisins are the reason.
You have ants in your pants or a bee in your bonnet or a luna moth in your
          loincloth.
You determine that there have been picked circumstances or extenuating
          beets, corduroy blackouts or rolling slacks, strawberry differences or an
          irreconcilable tart, hat fever or a hay trick, taffy shelter or a no-kill pull,
          rodeo feelings or a hard clown, ceramic glances or a sidelong glaze,
          concrete broth or a chicken poem, reasonable mouth or mealy doubt.
Your pencil is broken or your pen is leakin' your Aunt Carla ain't Lorca or
          Uncle Louis isn't Catullus and fuzzy wuzzy wasn't jazzy has no knack
          for bugling has he taxi your artsy, or bus you bass, bust your bassoon,
          I stubbed my tubas!, beg Mr. Music for the cornets and the lieder or sorry
          hummingbird there are hornets at the feeder.

table for one
the way she stirs her tea
in tight circles

SUZANNE ROBERTSON

SOFT SPOTS

Clouds that have triumphed in their push-up bras

Bare kneecaps, violinists, anyone who works
in charcoal

The gold bands that keep slipping off
our second tallest fingers

Reverend what's-his-name who lifted his arms at Cliff's
funeral and gave us free admission to the membership

Chlorophyll and Jesus

Rain, old tape recorder rain

The man when he shuts his hole, puts the beer
down, removes his TV glasses and stares
out the window like a Labrador

That park bench off Cumberland

Anyone who makes room for crazy

The old woman who vacuums the tall grass
of her carpet

The shadow lands my father made against
the wall with his hands

His hands

The way stethoscopes feel against your inner language

Woolf and wolves

Cats who know they were born to be secret agents

Duck tails on humans

Swans when they take off their masks in my dreams

The psychiatrist who will not sleep tonight

The gardener's sage-scented fingers on the stem
of my worry

Kukus that terrorize the Jacaranda trees on the road
to Kilimanjaro

The boy who grins like a platypus, his handwriting Prochesy,
Peter, Bolo, the way he walks around the orphanage
like a car salesman

The man praying on the rooftop at dawn, the mosque
made of bedsheets, my hotel room no bigger than
a lunch box where God touched
the soft spot

Anyone who rubs my earlobes for good luck

Anyone who can remember the words
to the Rainbow Connection

Anyone with a frog caught in their throat

SUSAN MUSGRAVE

MOTHER'S DAY BEHIND THE WEST HOTEL

If I had a choice I wouldn't be
a heroin addict; I'd get up each day
and do something different.
I'd be a mother to my daughter,
that would be enough for me.

I wanted to be a teacher, or an actress
but most of all a mother. I didn't want to be
a heroin addict, I said I would never
stick needles in my arms or let any man
make a bitch out of me. My goal was to be
a good mother, not like the mothers I had.

I'd want my daughter to speak her feelings,
say them out loud. I'd teach her to cry
but only if she wanted to. Heroin
doesn't let you do that. It hurts *for* you.

It thinks for you, it lives for you,
it fucks for you. It has no passion
except for you. It has no God but you.

It takes up in you, pushing you down
making you small. And when you're so small,
no bigger than the light from a match someone
strikes in the dark, the person you love
most could strike a match on your soul
and it wouldn't make you flinch.

SUSAN DRAIN

ALICE

Alice did not dance.
Her mouth twitched downward, froze there.
Her arm was
crook-
ed, and her hand a claw –
a stroke condemned her, trapped her,
penned her.
Just forty, with two young boys
at the foot of her bed
aghast
at the familiar woman redrawn
askew.
Speechless, all three.
She clawed herself back:
to walk, to talk, to smile – but not quite straight.
Held her right arm in an invisible sling,
turned up curled fingers to make a pocket,
a place to wedge and hold and brace whatever needed
two good hands.
And her left hand learned to write
when letters were the only tie
between her soldier sons
and home.
Sometimes I write with my left hand –
to be ready
should words be struck out of me.

CONTROL

The city: we are its muscle memory,
its reflex, instinct, its trapped animal self.
We are the leg it would gnaw off to escape.
The ambulance siren wails, open-mouthed,
helpless. Calling us.

We're formed by split-second decisions—this or that—
and have the rest of our lives to wonder about them.
Meanwhile, in every neighbourhood,
behind every door, the silent hum of survival:
fridges wait in halos of static, dogs sleep
like bees in the hive. Seldom can we inhabit
the mystery we are, our houses shut against doubt.
We breathe in, try to reassure ourselves,
tighten our belts another notch.

SUE

SUE MACLEOD

THIS IS A POEM WHERE WORDS ARE THE UNDERPAID WORKERS

This is a poem
for the helping words: if, and, or, in, to…
written in sympathy
for their cause, their desire
to step out from the shadow
of the rushing verbs, the nouns as fat
as capital. This is for weeknights
when helping words gather in the basement
of the local church:
"My name is The, and I'm a co-dependent."

This is about the uncelebrated power
of words like these. About telling
the truth, or *a* lie. Going home; going
into a… home.

This is a poem where words
are the underpaid workers
who give you a sponge bath, and bring the small articles
you call for. The ointment. The bedpan.
A little something to make you
more comfortable. They're the ones whose tenderness
or cruelty matters
in those hours
before your body becomes
"the body." It is their cushion soles your loved ones follow
down the corridor—"this way, please"—
to claim you, in the end.

SUSAN IOANNOU

THE LISTENERS

Waking in northern darkness,
we grope from tree to tree.
Above, the branches are woven so thick
no stars wink through—we only remember
a black dome over moon-shivered water
netted with lights so clear
they would have lit our way
along this rotting surveyors' swath
iridescent with lichen on long-downed trunks
where feet sink into mould and moss.

What else, beside us,
creeps among trees unseen?
We strain at every snap and rustle
until as shadows shift and thin,
from a distant greying branch
a faint chirp,
a *chickadee-dee*
and in answer
chirrups and *cheeping*.

As birches redden,
high in glistening cedar and pine
more and more tiny throats swell the throbbing
with joyous vibrations to welcome dawn
until we, too, like aspen are shivering
that each day—with or without us—goes on
this ancient celebration: returning the light.

Read by Lea Harper to the participants in her Haliburton Trails and Tours walk, October 16, 2004.

KINDRED KINE

Two lopsided cows
knuckle-kneed
flick droning flies
and lick each other's
wind-weathered sides,
capsizing at dusk
under the hill.

Two heads lift
as a woman passes.

Grooming resumes,
joint leanings
one into the other,
a shelter of tongues.

Who is to say these companions
inclining toward dark
do not move those soft tongues
against the day of their slaughter?

SUSAN GLICKMAN

ON FINDING A COPY OF *PIGEON* IN THE HOSPITAL BOOKSTORE
for Karen Solie

I prowled the rows of the hospital bookstore with a fevered intensity;
"fevered" because it was a hospital, "intensity" because I was perplexed by
the mysteriously ruptured tendon in the middle finger of my right hand
in sympathy with which the whole hand had cramped
so that I could scarcely hold a pen or open a jar.
Even a five-month-old octopus in the Munich zoo can open a jar!

The octopus's name is Frieda, which reminded me
of D.H. Lawrence, and thinking of him
brought me to the hospital bookstore. It was minimally stocked
with anything resembling literature, offering those in pain,
afraid, or just dully waiting for test results
a choice of pink-jacketed chick-lit, cookbooks, investment guides
or glossy thrillers spilling blood
as red as that pooling down the hall in the O.R.
as though emulating some homeopathic principle
of curing a disease by a parody of that which caused it.

And perched as eccentrically as the sparrow who sings from the rafters
at Loblaws, and looking just as lost,
was the only volume of poetry in the store.
Reading it I recognized at once what I disliked
about the bulky bestsellers nudging it from the shelf
like bullies in the halls of high school, their meaty faces
full of self-regard, their minds absent of thought.
I hate the omni-present present tense, that fake cinematic contrivance
meant to create a sense of "being in the moment" with the hero
as though life were a constant rush of adrenaline
with no possible mood but surprise.

Whereas poetry offers the results of its meditation
tentatively; it is not embarrassed to show that thinking
—some of it slow, arduous, confused — has taken place.
And then poetry doesn't rush ahead shouting, "Look at me! Look at me!"
Instead, it takes your hand, your poor mangled hand, like the good surgeon it is
and massages it joint by joint, feeling for the sore places.
And because it doesn't speak without reflection
you trust it, and let it cut you open.

SUZANNAH SHOWLER

A SHORT AND USEFUL GUIDE TO LIVING IN THE WORLD

Take, say, the roster of details worried into a day
like grit in unlaundered wool:

> Bridge, spinal-thin, trellised over tracks to lift and keep you presiding over
> some take on a city's spread

> Mottled wet of early morning's pavement oily, slick as an animal hide

> Paper jammed in the outbound roller tray inking out strains like an overnight
> drift off unwashed eyelashes

> Staircases laced with violated building codes

Re-camp these entries along new lines,
unearth the secret alliances between them.
There is much work to be done, each instant
cleft open like a horizontal fluke.

Spend time loitering, slipping coins into attention's slots,
anticipating the next big pay-off.

When you tire of this, you can mouth a word
until the seam of its meaning splits open.
(Try *goulash*. Try *transmogrify*.)

Ask or be asked: *which way does the ballerina spin?*
Use your hours trying to catch the image on its axis,
shadow flipping over shadow, and think to yourself:
you'll dizzy your senses on all the things you didn't choose.

The trick is to try to live in earth-time
and keep the vigil of an orbit around anything.

Employ these and other strategies that prove useful.

Please write to me of your success.

SUSAN ELMSLIE

SEVEN LETTERS TO MY MOTHER
7. PISCES, YOU SWIM IN TWO DIRECTIONS

No letter for some time.
Frustration kept me from sending them
when they go unacknowledged,
when I meanly imagine them piled, gathering dust
in the dead-letter office of your mind.
Each bright stamp glazing over
like the eyes of fish washed up on the beach.
Yes, melodramatic.
I felt it.

Hunger abates when the body's denied
food or contact; we stumble
on for some time, throttling its alarms.
You used to rip the batteries out of the smoke detector
when the broiling cod set the red eye shrieking.

Apparently I am still my own child.

But now bad news comes
almost as a relief, makes it easier
to cast out another line
so to speak. The doctor gave your silence a name:
Alzheimer's—a kind of organized forgetting.

When did it start?
Each of us swimming in two directions
like the symbol for our sign of the zodiac,
and the fish in the song I'd beg you to sing

when I was three: *swim said the mama fish, swim*
if you can—
This moment

I'm rounding up memories
scattered as the beads of a broken choker
and as luminous:
a diver leaping from the lip of a cliff
105 feet high in Acapulco,
where you honeymooned with Dad;

your baby squinting into the sun
for a photograph on the sidewalk
of the new subdivision;
sisters-in-law laughing over an all-night game of cards
at the kitchen table, rum & coke and smoke
hanging in the air with the bawdy talk;
and after Dad left, summers
browning your shoulders on the front porch
with a detective mystery or Linda Goodman's *Sun Signs*.

This moment I swim to you.

SUE GOYETTE

A COLLAGE OF SEASONS FOR A GRIEVING WIDOW

November days crumble into underground stairways
with winding halls and regrets flickering
like candlelight. Outside, paths have disappeared

beneath snow; you have only familiar trees now
to guide you. And you're lost in the night
between winter and spring that lies

like a clarinet in its case
waiting. Only the empty sky is loud, craving
crocuses and even just a sliver of moon.

　　　　❧

It takes you all summer to toughen
your bare feet on the leering beach rocks before the sea.
And you still comb the week before he died for that one glittering word

of warning, a word so thin and sharp
it's sliced these August days in two, full of gardens
he never planted and dishes that must be washed.

　　　　❧

The sun is slower in September. It catches
in the birches and warms plump squash
resting on thin vines, it even splashes

your double bed that grows a little every night.

And when afternoons cloud with smoke from burning leaves,
you dream at night of blizzards, of not being

able to see your hand held out
in the snow. The hand that slowly
is becoming his face.

SUSAN HALDANE

ALTAR CALL

You might
from time to time feel
a slight stirring:
the sermon wrapped up
tight, yeasty smell of dread
and anticipation rising,
the first chord of Just As I Am
dragging across hand-worn pew backs:
Just as I am, without one plea
But that thy blood was shed for me.
With the organ's weighty soundtrack
the preacher bids the sinful forward:
Just as I am and waiting not
To rid my soul of one dark blot.

Every week's the same script
and he's calling
you or some other serial confessor,
forgiveness junkie
kneeling at the rail
for that short sweet hit
of reverent love,
absolute absolution,
the preacher's wings over you
sweat-slicked foreheads bent,
oh, and his familiar verbal tic,
asking just this Lord, just that;
"just fill him up, Lord"
as if that were
no great thing.

Just as I am, though tossed about
With many a conflict, many a doubt,
Fightings and fears within, without,
O Lamb of God, I come.
He seems to want so badly
your contrition, your tears
and you are
tempted,
balanced there,
fear of the fires weighing
earth-bound embarrassment and
the wondering eyebrows of the righteous.
O lamb of God
I come, I come.

But you don't
come. Avoiding the crash, the fall, this week you resist and again
next week you harden your heart. Sunday on Sunday
you sit, you quit
cold turkey, and
finally
you do not hear the call
at all.

SUSAN PADDON

CHIRRUP, CHIRRUP

There is a dog disturbing
a magnificent brown finch in the magnolia.
Bromide! I call. Even in my dreams
there is Anton Chekhov. The steppe
outside my window

cold as all hell.

In the dream, the dog doesn't answer, but a stirring inside
my mother's house reminds me
I've been far away and I must get back.

It is my mother who is closer to Chekhov. The wings inside her,
changing like the peppered moth.

I am more Masha. The sister,

who keeps secret watch,
notes blood on pillow casings.
I've read every cough he ever wrote, only
in my dreams they always seem to get better.

There's this recurring vision of a boy
who jumps foxholes on the steppe, who walks,
coat open, in the rain.

SUSAN MCMASTER

LEARNING TO FORGET

The fourth year, she returns
to the half-done dressing table.
Rinses the dishes, leaves them for me
to put away on the shelves.
Waves to the neighbours.
Cheerfully says, "I don't remember."
Greets me as my sister,
laughs when she finds I'm me.

They said this would happen,
the friends who console us -
a short, happy state
when she would stop fighting,
learn how to forget.

In between, there are hours
when we talk as we used to.
Neither of us hears
me repeat names and facts
over and over
and over.

SUE MACLEOD

AN UNMARRIED WOMAN CONSIDERS COLVILLE AND HIS WIFE

Thirty-three years between *Woman in Bathtub* and
Woman Climbing a Ramp,
coming out of the ocean—

No one will know me like this.

This isn't envy,
not exactly. Not with Colville
lurking, looking ominous in his robe.

Her nipples are the only warm colour.

She is

       woman doing headstand
       woman with revolver
       woman taking bath…

The water demarcates her
legs like ankle socks,
recalls a time before even he

had seen her.
Her pubic hair rises above shoreline:
well-treed island

and her hand, submerged—
a submarine, a shark, a separate consciousness.

She is now

an old woman, in bathing suit,
holding both rails.
He paints

the hang of loose flesh
on her arm. He paints how low
her breasts have fallen.

Is she thinking, *look away for once*
or is she stopped
as I am

by the heat
seeping in to later Colvilles
and because he's got it right again:

the delicate detailing
of collarbone,
how this is not diminished.

A shadow falls to one side like a cape
and she's reaching

out of it.
And—this is envy, exactly—
she's still a swimmer. He is still her witness.

Who else could see her in this light?

SUSAN STENSON

READER RESPONSE THEORY

the woman is running down the road
past the yellow house
and if the line above had read walking
it would be a very different poem

what if the woman was crawling down the road
past the yellow house but the house was not really yellow
because yellow is not a colour of houses in this town
so it must really be a jail with yellow bricks and grey mortar,
the colour of jails in this town and the woman is running or walking
or crawling past it so the road easily becomes
the road you were running on that day you ran past the yellow house
but had to make it look like you were really walking so nobody'd get
any funny ideas and realize you were not running down the road past
the yellow house at all but running away

from the yellow house and all that time it felt like you were crawling
not running not walking, crawling, and what if
you were not a woman at all but a man running this road
the readers would need to know what kind of man you were because
men in poems are much harder to see

easy to see a woman running down the road past the yellow house
what kind of reader will question a woman running down the road
past the yellow house or assume she must have a reason for running
because the poem says she is running but the poem does not say that
she is running away from anything unlike you that time in stanza two

you were definitely running away from something so she
must be running away from it too and if the man was also
running down the road past the yellow house the reader
would want to know where the man was running to because
many readers will assume the man would be running toward
something and not away from anything but it's the woman
who is running down the road
past the yellow house and that is all you are told

SUSAN MCMASTER

LATELY, SHE REMEMBERS: MARCH

Her palms are hungry. Oh, other parts too, but in the night, now he's gone, and even the cat finds elsewhere to sleep, it is her palms that ache for the feel of his shoulder, right there, in the centre of her hand, where the bones come together, flesh sparks at a touch. The heart, she calls it to herself, much more real than the erratic muscle that lodges over her stomach, stutters when she climbs the stairs too fast, burns and knocks, a complaining roomer always ready to whine.

> *In the rain-pattered night she rubs palms against*
> *the sheet - his hip - his shoulder - how they fit as*
> *she rolls onto her side, as she smooths her hand*
> *down a muscled arm, slips it over her chest, circles,*
> *presses till the nipple hardens, tucks knees against*
> *thighs, soft fur rubbing as she strokes further down,*
> *strokes the curl of hair under the slow ribs, down*
> *the feathered belly, cups a soft rise.*

In the flat, empty bed, she covers her mouth, brings a tongue
into that crease. Cups her heart.
Licks it dry.

SUSAN MUSGRAVE

ALL THE WILD WINDS OF THE WORLD
GO HOWLING THROUGH YOU

as you write one more poem of longing
and send it shivering into the next world
because, inside you, it no longer has a home.

What do you expect -
to sit under the cedar trees
all day and come away the wiser?

Your boy on the winter beach knee-deep in foam,
laughing and stumbling towards his father's arms,
like the rest of us, perhaps, longing for home.

SUSAN GILLIS

INTERSECTION

Leaves were falling, and rain
in strings, nearly straight
down, gravity
doing its jig again, like the
irrepressible men in
the old fishers' home, mated
to the wheeling earth.
Dips in the street collected the rain.
the wet leaves fell
onto the street, wet,
onto the resonant lakes.
The leaves were slow
as duck feathers. I can say
"slow as duck feathers"
whether I've seen
duck feathers falling
or not, because
we are in a blind. Watch now:
a man is about to walk by with a creel
and a woman will cross holding a black umbrella.
They are not related and will not meet,
except in the rain and the leaves.

SUSAN OLDING

WHAT WE THOUGHT ABOUT THE CHINESE MOTHERS *

We tried not to think. We tried to pretend
they didn't exist. We thought about paint chips—

we picked colours for the nursery,
we thought about cribs and baby monitors.

The bellies of pregnant women bothered us,
so we ignored them. We shopped for socks,

sleepers and bottles, suitable gifts
to bring the *ayis*—make-up, we were told,

take them eyeliner and lipstick—but that
advice seemed suspect, since even the best

brands bore the label *Made in China*. We
packed our suitcases, renewed our passports,

filled out forms and got our shots. Some of us
studied Mandarin, but most decided

not to. We didn't want to know the details—
how they spoke about their shame or fear.

We knew they were oppressed by law;
that made their choice impersonal

and we preferred to let it seem
that way. We refused

to plant imagination
in their windswept rice fields, could not bear

the thought of giving birth to sorrow.
An inkwash ponytail or the play of pearls on skin

might prompt the question—*will my daughter look
like that?* But mostly we thought of ourselves.

* *With thanks to Rachel Rose, who invented this form, which she calls the "pas de deux."*

SUSAN OLDING

WHAT THE CHINESE MOTHERS SEEMED TO THINK ABOUT US

They tried to pretend we didn't exist.
Showed or feigned ignorance when told

about the orphanages hulking just outside
their cities' walls. They defended the one-child

policy, said it made their country strong
and those who gave birth over-quota should

be punished. They thought we were fat, too big
and too big-nosed, unbeautiful—though rich.

They thought we meant their children harm,
thought we'd treat them as slaves and never tell them

about their Chinese past. They thought we were
fools for taking trash that someone else had wisely left

to die. They thought we were saints. They thought
the babies were lucky, they thought we

were lucky. Time was short. They did their best
to teach us how to dress the infants,

their fingers fumbling with buttons and socks
to cover the skin we'd left bare. They served

us meals, cleaned our rooms, assembled the cots
the babies slept in. If their eyes grew damp

at the thought of so many children leaving
their shores, their faces were smooth as folded linen.

SUSAN ELMSLIE

LUMP

The gowns have got better over the years.
They used to be papery. Putting them on
made you feel a little like fast food.
Now at least they're soft washed cotton, though
this one smells exactly like a taco shell.
I've pulled my arms out of it, and am lying on my back,
staring at the underbellies of wooden tropical fish
on a mobile over my head. Two of each kind, I see:
a pair of blue and white ones with purple flashes,
two seaweed and amber ones, a fiery orange and purple pair. Only
one pink one, though. Rare fish low in the murky water.
It's pea-sized, the doctor is saying, picking up my hand
and pressing my fingers to it, deep
in my left breast beside the nipple, *at 8:00*. She lands my hand there
with such force I feel like I am pressing the elevator button
for the second time. I'm reminded
also, more vaguely still, of someone I saw smooshing a dog's nose
in poop on the living room carpet, the words *bad dog*.
I never would have found that, I say, partly in defence, partly
in awe. My fingers rest dutifully there a moment,
as if I were making a pledge.
Then I scuttle upright on the table, wrap the robe around me.
Any history in your family? the doctor wants to know.
My granny's sister lost a breast to cancer.
Then there are quick calculations related to my cycle,
caffeine consumption, age. My mind
starts to shut down with the introduction of the words,
ultrasound, biopsy, Urgent Breast Clinic.
I've gone under, swimming in my deep blue robe,

my head sounds like a seashell, a churning undertow.
The walk to the bus stop I catch myself involuntarily
saying words out loud: *never; tired; clay*, now and then
punctuating my disbelief with hand gestures
straight out of silent film. So the crazy ladies
are just worried, I intuit, jabbing
the air with its unseen buttons.
Later, on the phone long distance, my mother
tells me that she wonders whether Auntie's lump
didn't come about because, years earlier, she caught
her breast in the wringer washer real bad.
How such things may be related who can predict?

    Earlier this summer my neighbour chased off an addict
    who was at the recycling bins on his back deck,
    fishing for returnable empties in the murky 4 a.m. light. I woke up
    to hear the young securities dealer warning the interloper:
    I'll give you a lump—I'll lump ya if you come back here.
    Months ago, waking up in the dark to this hard-boiled threat, I laughed
    out loud, easily, safe under layers: night-gown, down comforter.

SIOUX BROWNING

THE PERFECT TEN

I want a man who will wear a baseball cap
every day of his life-long past the time
when his last strand of hair has fallen out.

I want a man for whom the four food groups
are meat and potatoes, barley and malt.

I want a man with a cherry red 4 by 4
jacked up to the point that I need a ladder to get in it,
with fuzzy seats and blue sex lights lining the dash
and a hockey stick in the gun rack.

I want a man who will take me mud-bogging,
or at the very least to the monster truck exhibition
down at the stadium.

I want a man who will call me 'mother' at home and
'the little woman' around his friends;
who will pat me on the butt in public and announce
I seem to be gaining a few.

I want a man who is not afraid to let his Molson muscle
hang over the front of his Speedos;
who will wander around the house in his underwear
with his hand stuck down the front, scratching absently
as he looks for the T.V. Guide.

I want a man who refers to motorcycles as crotch rockets,
who thinks a romantic proposal is, "Hey baby, let me slip
you my hot beef injection,"
who cleans his fingernails with his teeth,

and who can hit any moving dog at thirty paces by flicking
a twist cap by his ear.

I want a man who thinks Jean-Claude Van Damme is an
acting tour de force.

I want a man who thinks tour de force is a bicycle race in Europe.

I want this man because he is so hard to find. His kind
all seem to be taken by women luckier than me.
Women who didn't waste their time looking
for someone better, first.

SUNDOWNING

I remembered it this morning:
tiny disk, orange, in my palm,
my lifeline a rickety horizon.
I'd been restless last night,
I was told, and made to sleep --
that is, I lay oblivious, blind
fetus in a fur-lined rabbit's nest.

Now the surface again. Bleached
tile of daylight. Hours till dusk
descends. I must not tip my hand.
Yesterday, I rocked in my chair
at dinner, saw through the drapes'
crack: there the sun's fontanelle
brow, its fevered downward thrust.

I only yelled because the vermilion-
apricot soft in its wake exploded
into electric blue, emerald, cerulean,
teal. My legs warmed by ejected heat,
the earth's crust thinning beneath
my shoes as I was coaxed back
into my room. My bones filaments.

Tonight, I plead illness, sip broth
in bed, boots shrouded under sheets;
I'll slip outside, watch for that lava
flash; then run, body flaring free
of flesh, to lapis lazuli waters,
green crowning beyond the curve.

SUSAN GLICKMAN

AFTER PASTERNAK

A man walking through fields at turn of season
forgets his life:
what he says about it when his feet are squared under a table
and everyone's talking too fast,
or how he lines up those memories by his bed each night
like shoes he will step into in the morning.

Hills under the purple blur of autumn
are something he has never seen before.
White horse running for joy
hooves ploughing the ice-curdled earth—
it asks no questions.

The sky stung by crows into sudden clamour
beyond the far fringe of branches;
black feathers sloughed from the ascending moon.

And the way small pools in the mud,
so many dark eyes,
wink up at him as he walks past,
crossing over from then to now as though
it were the easiest thing in the world.

SUSAN MUSGRAVE

YOU DIDN'T FIT
for my father

You wouldn't fit in your coffin
but to me it was no surprise.
All your life you had never fit in
anywhere; you saw no reason to
begin fitting now.

When I was little I remember
a sheriff coming. You were
taken to court because your
false teeth didn't fit and you

wouldn't pay the dentist. It was
your third set, you said none of them
fit properly. I was afraid then
that something would take you from me
as it has done now: death
with a bright face and teeth that
fit perfectly.

A human smile that shuts me out.
The Court, I remember, retuned
your teeth, now marked an exhibit.
You were dismissed with costs—
I never understood. The teeth were
terrible. We liked you better
without them.

We didn't fit, either, into your
life or your loneliness, though you
tried, and we did too. Once
I wanted to marry you, and then left;
I'm still the child who won't fit
into the arms of anyone, but is
always reaching.

I was awkward for years, my bones
didn't fit in my body but stuck out
like my heart—people used to comment
on it. They said I was very good
at office parties where you took me
and let others do the talking—the
crude jokes, the corny men—I saw
how they hurt you and I loved you
harder than ever

Because neither of us fit. Later you
blamed me, said "You must fit in,"
but I didn't and I still think
it made you secretly happy.

Like I am now: you won't fit in your
coffin. My mother, after a life
of it, says, "This is the last straw."
And it is. We're all clutching.

SUSAN TELFER

PORTRAIT

Painted in oil from a photo, looking
as if I have confidence.
On canvas, I'm unsmiling.
More still a girl, really, at ten.
Where is that milk-blood boundary line—
the minute between woman and girl?
My long hair a veil down my spine,
a shield from the too overt world.
She watches me—fierce, forlorn—
from the mystery of her wild nature.
For what purpose was she born?
Would I go up to her, with what gesture
could I reach her, my palimpsest, at all?
I can hardly bear to hang her on the wall.

SUE SINCLAIR

CLAIMED

You know it's no use being attached to things, but
even when the worst has happened, is happening,
the little animal of the heart keeps digging
further into the earth.

You don't want to give up even heartbreak,
even death, the peace that comes in deep pain
when you have no way out.

The insects, the summer heat, declare themselves through you;
you are claimed
and so commit yourself to the blood of this place:
      a rhythmic stillness, a buzzing,
everything in the world
brimming with loneliness
and the sunlit presence of its demise.

SUSAN BRISCOE

SABOTEURS

Your complaint: invisibility. It *is* hard to see you
across the hectares of corn leeching the lowlands

between this hill and the city squatting in its river—
I argue, just to win. Were I honest, I'd admit

to being deaf as well as blind. We have become abstractions.
A theory of opposites. Or, a conversation

looped back on itself, the half-twisted telephone wire
a Mobius strip. Certainly, this is not the way it is done.

The distance between each side of our marital bed reaches
a hundred thousand metres, from baked urban brick

to cool Appalachian wood,
across every binary we could think of. Saboteurs,

we two, stretching our tenuous bond
like my boys their elastics, aimed at the eyes.

SUE SORENSEN

FREUD AND JUNG IN AMERICA, 1909: CONEY ISLAND

Not only that, but the first film they have ever seen. Dinner at Hammerstein's Roof Garden. Central Park. Contortionists, show girls, the 1909 equivalent of the hot dog. Later, Niagara Falls, intestinal trouble for Freud, an uneasiness about American manners. Which, apparently, they haven't got.

America is distrustful. Freudian theory is sensational, too sexual, and yet, when Freud doesn't bring up sex, they are peeved. Jung decides around this time to sidestep the sexual problem. Perhaps the high point for Freud is finding that the cabin steward on the ship to America is reading one of his books. For Jung was it analyzing on board his mentor's dreams, probing the relation to wife and wife's sister? Jung says: Freud is touchy.

Freud's authority is under siege. He allows himself to be vulnerable. A blunder. He is promised three thousand marks for the lectures at Clark, but they are not yet written. He walks outdoors with his friend Ferenczi, writing and planning aloud, composing on the move. Somewhere in Europe Zeppelin is trying to fly, and Orville and Wilbur do the same in America.

At home, later, he predicts, as a dour half-joke, that over there blacks will replace whites. *It serves America right.*

The Hotel Manhattan, where they stay for two-fifty a night, no longer exists. Torn down in the sixties for a mediocrity. You like to imagine the maids at the Hotel Manhattan wrinkling noses at the cigar smoke. The elevator boys waiting for his *Danke.*

When he breaks with Jung in 1913, he thinks that Jung has tried too hard to *liberate mankind from the hardship of sex.* It cannot be done. But anyone who tries? *Hailed as a hero*, he says.

SUE MACLEOD

THE GOD OF POCKETS

The God of Pockets smiles on children.
On their thumb-polished chestnuts. And what She,
in her benevolence, sees as their innocent
lint. She sees the lucky penny
drop, knows the hunger
of keys. Knows what the landlord has tallied
on his calculator. Knows the man who sleeps
outside the library. In particular, the flattened
pack of smokes
against his chest. She's held
the knife that carved
the crooked
heart into the tree trunk. The referee's whistle.
The mickey of gin. The wallet, and the picture
in the wallet, and the smile
in the picture. The finally unbearable weight
of a gun
in its holster. Weight of a secret, held in.
She's the god of tide pools. Of harmonicas.
Marsupials. A mother
bounding forty miles an hour
through the flatlands, joey
leaning out over the edge. She knows the way
to a ten-dollar bill
tucked in last winter's coat
on a flat-broke day in spring—like one more
thing that time's forgotten. And on bright days
when the swing sets and the iron rails
of the monkey bars throw shadows, tall as

office towers spreading to the outback,
the God of Pockets speaks
to children. Run, She says. Take
what you can.

Susan Glee

Susan Stevenson

Suzette Mayr

Sue Parr

Sue McMaster

Sue S. Olson

Susan Ioannou

Susan Siddeley

SUZIE

Sue

Susie Petersiel Berg

CONCEPTION

In a circle of reeds at the marsh's edge
there is a turn-around, a pedestal of dirt
dumped from construction sites and leveled,
its surface etched with scroll work where tires come
and turn and stop. Nightly, cars rest here,
windows creamy with condensation and lit
with the green glow of radios which press
the muzzy beats of Booker T against the glass.
Every now and then the cop car makes a pass,
causing a flurry of straightened slips, pant legs
snagged on stick shifts and caught breath.
But days the place is empty, a disregarded jetty
the muskrats cross to slip into the rushes.
A mallard hen snaps at the short grass, constructing.
Some small current pushes a froth of bubbles
against the shore. Today, rain patters the icy water
and a car, green, with cardboard strapped to the grill
to stop the cold, turns off the road from town.
Gravel pops against the undercarriage.
The man and the woman inside look at each other
startled, as if the percussion of it might scare
the other off. They are both grateful
when the car stops. Some minutes of conversation
make the bridge from where they've come —
the coffee shop in Woolworth's; their cups
still resting on the table, his tea bag neatly pressed
against his spoon, a scatter of sugar near her plate —
to where they are. How it's still so cold for April.
Has she always lived here? She hears the drawl

in his voice, the way it lengthens her name
for just a moment, and decides that the gas office
can wait for once, she's never late and besides,
today it isn't busy. He watches her gesture, birdlike,
and thinks how Classical her profile is.
His broad thumb caresses the bridge of her nose,
her eyes the colour of the grey afternoon.
Her hands slip around his back.
The space inside the car cinches them together,
compresses them into an indrawn breath, the smell
of new lingerie purchased from the Merc., the taste
of Earl Grey tea with lemon, and an urgent want.
Both of them strain to reach a warm place
inside the other. Achieve it.
Then the space inside the car expands again.
They slip apart.
Some sound nearby flushes the mallard
from her half-finished nest. She spins into the sky,
brown wings churning through the rain.
On looking down, she sees the patterned water,
the islands of grass, a scallop of snow against the shore.
She sees the car below her and recognizes it as an egg,
its shell iridescent and wet. She wonders what bird
might warm an egg so large and what bird might emerge
from it. She sees it as a thing which will eventually
be broken. She turns in the air and descends again,
having forgotten now what ever lifted her.

SREBRENICA SUITE

3. The Abandoned Hospital

Bone-withered,
their eyes are like peeled eggs
turning black, and back
inside half-emptied skulls.

Fingers, red lumps puffed with cold,
cannot hold even tatters
over transparent skin.

Pieces of selves, not people,
their fireworked nerves shudder.
Above, the fractured moon
dangles its sparking cord.

4. Survivor

Each night,
a black-scarved woman
squats by the riverbank.

Her small net
splashes and crawls
—a boot? a bone?

Behind,
barbed wire
catches the moon.

SUE SINCLAIR

WINTER IN THE GARDEN

Everything sleeps.
The serpent curls round the roots of the apple tree,
which is bare. The leaves have not gone, but have changed
into thought. Fallen apples lie under a bed of snow.
In spring they'll rise into the branches again.
Meanwhile they dream, sometimes of the legendary chunk of apple
carried down to Earth in Eve's stomach, which sends back
messages to its brothers and sisters. *I'm coming home,*
soon. It has learned some things
it can't talk about. In jobless towns along the US-Mexico border
40% of the young men want to be hired assassins.
What can Eden find to compare to this?
Wanting to lead *some* kind of life
while it's still possible. Maybe the blaze of sun across the snow,
maybe that. But not the drip, drip, drip of the melt
as paradise wakens. Not the bright sky.
Nothing that has not had to die.

BEDTIME STORIES

Inverted, we lie
in circles of
lamplight.
His body straight
as an intention.
I curl into and
along his length.
Space between
the text fills
with skin-scent;
twilight in a lather,
scrubbed fresh.
Rhythm pinned
to the pages,
words in fixed order.
Their steady rollick
a subset of down,
nape and neck.
We syncopate breaths,
catch time in
butterfly nets.
Hush now the moon,
the great green room,
these seas I'd gladly drown for.

SUE WHEELER

COLD HANDS

The thin gloves fished out of last year's jacket
pocket don't seem to do the job today.
It must be the fault of my heart,
storing summer's heat, reheated by the coals
each grief has dropped. Hearth, heart, heat —
the difference a letter makes, for instance
the one this morning that said
I thought you'd want to know...
Oven mitts may be what's needed
to handle a heart in this condition.
Boxer's gloves, though I've recently quit
saying to life, *Put up yer dukes.*
When I was a child, no lady would go downtown
sans nylons, heels and gloves. I'd like to be the woman
whose sent-to-her-room daughter tossed a note
that read *I hat you.* The woman who would fold
that note into a paper air
plane and scribble
the answer on a wing: *I glove you.*

SUZETTE MAYR

BIRDIE THE DOG IN REPOSE

My dog hobbles from arthritis, her anus sloppy and urethra dripping and protruding. Mini-strokes have leaned her directions to the left. Why won't you die? I scrub away a rotten peach stool from the wood floor, the yoga mat under the pillow she sleeps on, sponge her ass. Please don't die. Sadness a hammock. But she is a recurring character in my dreams, her black fur coat and bent legs, toes coiling from age. I am an evil daughter. She is white-haired Oma old, running in her sleep, her ankles flicking, sleep-walking yelps throw from her throat. She curls into dog fetus, a crescent, a croissant, a fingernail moon. Please die, don't die, her limbs and flicking pupils invaded with stroke, perpetual left lean, her body gradually curling into a fingernail moon. On good days, she sits, front paws crossed, manners delicate as a porcelain dragon's.

SUSAN PADDON

ROOM 45, HOTEL DRESDEN, MOSCOW

I like to imagine
peacock wallpaper and starched sheets. The bathroom
down the hall.

Before they married, it was their meeting place
each time he came to the city.

And if she got there first, straight from rehearsal, did she stand,
shoulders back, before the long dusty mirror to practise not being Arkadina
for a while. Her hair let loose at the temples
like a pair of ribbons. She rubbed rose water
on her knees and feet.

On the way up, two lemonades, he might have told the bellboy, and
a kopeck not to return again that evening. Did he stop each time
on the landing to catch his breath,

hoping to hear a quarrel down the hall, before going in. It was such a long
journey from the south.

I know how she would have undressed him,
slowly at first (he wore so many layers). They climbed under the white
of the white sheets. Outside, the city fast asleep.

And how many times he must have almost whispered,
with his nose pressed to the back of her,

they had everything

if wanting was enough.

SUSAN IOANNOU

BALKAN WINTER
(for Larry)

Ten years old,
inside the snow-crusted window, watching
over your neighbours' red-tiled roofs
you hear it
zing-zing
flashing in frost-bright air.

Beyond the emptied laneways, the moutain
rises, ice-hung vineyards thinning
higher and higher
—white quickens
black, as the slopes swarm.

Fleas could spring
and drop like that
except these specks
these echoing pops and cracks
dot the snow red.

Frozen into the window, watching
you will not flatten against the wall
but count the flashes of tracer fire
zing-zing
shattering tiles on your neighbours' roofs.

SUSAN ANDREWS GRACE

HYPATIA'S WAKE

Hypatia's Syllabus

Space around her body breathed, morning star a guide, particularities

mathematically true to navigation behind skin's veil.

Hypatia taught comfort in the elegance of integers,

uncovered mystery in sky and heart. Her students loved her

inclusion, many ways to regard the cosmos. No duality

too large to unify and proof never difficult

for death's friendly justice.

Since she taught students from everywhere in the known world and everywhere on the religious spectrum Hypatia may have inclusively employed ritual from them all.

SUSIE PETERSIEL BERG

I AM FROM
— *with thanks to Pat Schneider and George Ella Lyon*

I am from scrap metal

a taste for scotch and fishing but little money and less patience

the green house with the walnut and lilac trees, the needlepoint chair covers and the ruby wine glasses, my grandfather's pink apron and the green vinyl benchseat in the kitchen

separate seating and a kosher kitchen, waiting *Shabbos* dinner until the men return from *davening*; hours-long *seders* in Hebrew and all the songs at the back of the *Haggadah*; falling asleep in the sunroom before falling asleep on the drive back to Toronto.

I am from sterling silver salt cellars

three countries, the camps, seven languages, forged papers, one child sent to safety on a donkey cart, a second child an unwanted surprise in exile; the apple of her father's eye

Ostralenka-Paris-Madrid-Lisbon-Philadelphia-Montreal-Hamilton; a second round of medical school in yet another tongue

a house on the mountain, money, early onset and a fear of the knock at the door, of the Nazis of driving of shampooing of ordering in restaurants of forgetting what I am saying

After that, I don't know where I am from.

UNDERSTORY

To walk out of the field guide
and listen. To wait
for the world to approach with its dapple and hands.
Who are you?
Dreamer On A Short String.
Big Boots Clomping Through The Underbrush.
There's an understory here, shades
of meaning, tale told by a rock
signifying everything.

To open the grammar of being seen
and let the creatures name *you*.
Lover Who Begins To Notice.
Figure Of Speech.

SUSAN SIDDELEY

GEOGRAPHILIA

It lies before you,
a sheet of limpid blues, frail greens and soft browns,
occasionally, a slash of red.
Some wavy lines run parallel some don't.
You trace them wondering, what, why,
turn the pages, yellows, greys,
words, not always horizontal.
Geography; Mondays and Wednesdays.
Best when it's raining and the windows steam up
and girls bend, licking their lips as they outline, shade, label,
then lean back, weary of exploring, waiting for the bell.
But recess buns are dry, forgettable, you stay inside
locating your town, county,
measuring how far, deciphering
names curling round capes and firths,
along mountain backs and wandering rivers.

Decades later,
antipodal in Chile,
a dozy dog follows as you drive down dusty *calle O'Higgins*
Hop it, you hiss. He wags his tail, gives you that familiar
lineal grin you've fallen for so many times.
His coat is sparse, brown and dry as Andean slopes.
You look both ways, lean over, open the door
and say, Get in, dammit,
hoping there's disinfectant under the sink.
You know very well charm oozing from maps,
mongrels and men in bars
should be ignored.

9 liner

T Triple C tourniquet. 9-line. Role 3. jet to Germany. fight soldier fight. breathe.
hang on to tubes and wires. not twisted trips in dust. cobra traps. lash. the smash the
bloody grab the blast the blast. hideous misstep. fuck. IED. fucking fucking IED.
your limbs bleed. out. almost gone. O2, Sats, ICU chatter. radio net. 9 liner 9 liner
wheeze life- support. not Apache, not Black Hawk, Chinook, whook whook whook
whook whook, fast air over KAF. out of there. you must. hang on. breathe son
breathe. we wait we wait. will to live. will you to live. will you live. hang on hang on.
over the red desert. you're almost. gone. breathe son breathe. hang on.

9 liner – radio call for a medical evacuation
T Triple C – combat 1ˢᵗ Aid
Role 3 – advanced medical facility
IED – improvised explosive device
KAF - Kandahar Air Field

SUE SINCLAIR

DEVOTION
for W.R.

Long days spent forgiving fathers
for all they didn't know and couldn't protect us from.
As young men, backs slowly bracing to take on
an inherited weakness. *I don't know*, they said, frustrated
because they felt they had disappointed us
so much already, had fallen too quickly,
born on the steep side of a cliff.

The eyes of some were dangerous, power collapsing
and trying to preserve itself. Some wept like statues,
their own childhoods emerging
and staring helplessly at the world.

Now we just want another chance,
want to retrieve the something beautiful we sank
in them years ago, then set them free
like a net of fish, skins shining. Nothing we learn
can quite cure us of our desire to go there:
to the sandy bottom, where lucent shadows play
and a rusted lure still gleams.

SUSAN STEUDEL

NEW LIFE

The dead give way —
want to curl against you like a new life,

want to carry
the bowl with you and me in it.

A penny hidden in a teacup,
teacup turned upside down.

Where the lake was once. Evaporated.
A flame cups into wax
new phased
(faced).

SUSAN IOANNOU

THE COMFORT OF ELDERS

You are my buffer between
the whitened landscape beyond a window
and now.

A few hours higher,
you can see further
out over ice where the shore disappears.

Snowlight calms in your faces.
Blue drifts by, translucent
as untroubled eyes.

I know, if I wait
and crane on tiptoes,
one day

I may see you melted through glass
drifting away on the wind
like a shudder.

ORDINARY (2)

It is careless - how we
bear riches -
      ... ordinary — is it?
      as bread
my brisk ride
home
through leaves of gold,
green, to the family
table — it is rich
with chicken, tomatoes, juice
in a jug —
                        "How
Can I Keep from Singing?"
it, the tune we
careless children
learned —
                   how can I
do otherwise than carry
her, too, through it
      daily, my
riches, carry her care-
fully as a cracking bowl,
      keep her
with me, warm
her with my heat, feel
for her
how
        the ruffled cat pats
        my arm for a rub,

how
      hot air rushes
           from a baseboard vent,
how
      the window jewels
           crocuses, rich
           purple, blue on rags of snow —

Pass it all to her.
Ease it through her pearl shell of restless pain.
Pour it streaming in —

        like water warming the earth —

        which I cannot do.
           I cannot do.

SUSAN GEE

INSISTENCE

I gave you gravel bits and dried moss, fungus from a downed birch.
I put you on a path you could not see, dropped your darkness
on the table: scented, threadbare. I wanted
yarn of you to coil around, chronicles for keeping.

We drove the sea road, end road,
where stones were legend from another country,
where swallows ate the precious sky.

There were berries, (small) and rain.
There were thorns stuck to your fingers when I licked them clean.
The windshield was a cold breath, a screen I melted in you,
an argument you soon let go of.

Come, I said, *it calls us, wants us.*
I pushed my memories inside your hand, throbbing blue,
their small mouths open.

You were silent –
            reaching for the pit of your own past,
for the throat desire leans to in a small wind.

I gave you milkweed, loosestrife, a string that kept my pocket warm.
I was old and vanishing. I was envy on its last hunt.
You were the smell the land gives off in spring,
the silent grunt my belly yearned for.
I was peaked and then arrested,
fixed.

UNDONE

I long for you the ordinary,
a riot of girlfriends; small intimacies
and delights of burgeoning friendship,
not an older boy who picks you up
in his 'stang with gin,
but a harmless boy with a soft touch,
a tender boy like your brother.

And boring subway rides that end
where they're supposed to
with nothing happening in between
but blurry faces passing in the night,
not this man in gray sweats jerking
off on the seat across from you, his eyes
never moving from your delicate face,
nothing that makes you stagger onto the platform,
relieved but mad at yourself,
Should have never got on that train.

Long for you parties filled with laughter,
jokes and a make out session with someone
you have a crush on who likes you back,
but not a boy entering your body as if
banging his way into your house.
Uninvited.

SUE CHENETTE

ON SEEING *ERNANI* LIVE IN HD FROM THE MET

C'mon, pronto, let's go, the guy in the brown sweater
sings out as a camera moves in on the scene change.
Wagon's gonna come right here. A rolling curve
of stairs glides past. *That your last piece?*
Let's get a clamp on the seventh step – this
to a man with a tool belt who tests,
tinkers, tests; bolts the intersection. Now
women in overalls, with buckets, paint and brushes
and masking tape, scan the plywood
stone, squat to touch up scuffs. Below,
one man vacuums while another
follows looping slack cord.
A flat of shrubbery descends
to grow beside the staircase.

When Ernani, standing on those stairs,
stabs himself and falls;
when Elvira, plunging a knife into her breast,
collapses one step below;
when their hands reach, almost, almost …
then touch a moment, before they sink back,
dying, at the feet of villanous Silva,

I'm half-seeing, still, the guys
backstage in tee shirts and jeans, their deft
maneuvers, the struts and beams they carry —
like gut and bones beneath
a skin of gesture played on stage.
Like Verdi's buoyant rhythm — insistent
afterbeats urging the next bass note, pulsing
under whatever celebration or malice or menace,
whatever grief or pleading,
shapes the bel canto phrases.
                              The plot
could veer to anything: We're
bones and pulse,
our skein of gesture, the songs
we come to sing.

SUSAN STENSON

THE CRAZY MAPS

Mother dies in a hospital bed in Peterborough,
thirty miles north of where she was born.

The leaves turn and fall into snow, roads slippery tonight,
a storm of memory in the headlights and this one bullies

its way to centre stage. The truth: she's gone.
It's snowing. We can't find Father.

When he hears the news, he drives in circles,
lost in the cul-de-sacs south of the city, amazed

how streets he'd driven all his life narrow and disappear.
In his red car, window cracked an inch, smoke fumes

a thin line toward starlight. Cigarette after cigarette
dropped in the suburbs on the crazy maps of grief.

A stranger, arriving after midnight, can't say
where he's been, coat open, tie askew,

everybody thinking he was the one who would go first.
Silence replaces her and snow spins a requiem

outside the window with city lights fading
under full cloud, the first hours without her.

This early fall morning, October, no one speaks
of the future or of the past. We are stuck

in private thoughts, the swirl and pull of the season,
sounds we hear when we sleep, furnace, fridge, fact.

Surely, we had a hand in it. Surely, had we known
some other way to love, she would have made it home.

Jenner

Susan Chickerman

Sue

SR

Susan McCaslin

Sue Boyd M.

Susan Holbrook

Suzanne Bowness

Sue Sclar

SUZANNE

SUE KANHAI

NIGHT SWIMMING

His body breaks the water.
There is no more beautiful music.

On the dock, wet with moonlight,
I wait for his silken head to bob.

He calls, and for a moment
I forget. Swimming, he stitches

the open waters, creates a seam
where there was none.

We are no longer children. We envy them
their freedom, their discoveries, their flight.

How does leaving create such a specific music,
we struggle to understand it.

He says loss is tympanic, it
continues to sound beyond our hearing.

A body breaks the water. It is mine.
There is no more beautiful music.

SUSAN GLICKMAN

RUNNING IN PROSPECT CEMETERY (EXCERPT)

Browen Wallace
1945-1989

❧

Because I never said "goodbye" our conversation's unfinished
and this shames me, that I should have been
such a coward, *unpregnant of my cause*, and saying
nothing. Yes I know
the old routine—that we don't
acknowledge dying till we're forced to
so as not to give up hope—but
it's good, too, to cry together, to give up
not hope but pretence.

Because I'm not allowed to give up hope either
for myself, for my husband, for each month
our child evades us again and mourning must be resisted
again because
no one's actually died
and the pretence continues, continues, that this is
not terminal.

But infertility is another kind of death.
I remember as a child the thrill
of recognition when I understood that sometimes
doing *nothing* could be bad, that negligence
could be a crime. That's what this is,
this death of possibilities

we ignore
because it doesn't fit the known contours of grief
to mourn for one not born.
But in this, too, it resembles my missing of you

not only for who you were
but for the years I looked forward to
together, years I took for granted
to know you better in.

⌇

And hope is a drug, isn't it? The only one
you agreed to take after radiation failed
and the thing that had been small grew bigger, defiant
or simply oblivious, under the cover of your poor
burnt face.

At first, anyhow, the treatment hurt worse than the disease
but the doctors assured you your suffering
was worth it, as they always do, compulsive gamblers
that they are, risking nothing but a challenge
to their career average. Or, for the compassionate ones,

the human pain they try to rise above, of helplessness;
for which they console themselves by declaring
that if only you'd come to them earlier
that might have cured you. So that any error is always
the patient's, so that their magic transcends

our misery, so that they are responsible only
for success and never for failure.
Leaving us with such bewildered shame
we must do penance at their shrine, praying
that the deity who punished us with illness
will now cleanse our sinning bodies

through the ministrations of these sainted healers, these
deluded Lancelots, armoured in statistics,
charging across our skins with their scalpels in pursuit of
Death who always evades them

possessing our bodies as no lover or doctor
ever can. So that this seduction by hope simply defers the day
when we all, all lovers and doctors,
collapse gratefully in those arms
extended to us, patiently, since our birth.

SUSAN GILLIS

THE COMPANY OF SEALS

I stopped on the bridge between the city and home
to look over. A group of boys rolled past
on skateboards. One turned back,
"You all right?" (*oh yes, fine*, smile a little)
"Because you seem sad." (*Well yes
there's that*). The harbour nodded
and the cars sped, and after a minute he rumbled away.

It was a season of seals. All that fall
I walked with seals—along the causeway,
into town, through dreams,
while you were busy burning
behind the house. One day I watched one
roll to the surface, loll on its back and watch me.
No doubt it was hoping I'd throw it some fish.
It might as well have lit a cigar.
Its whiskers were long, and water
flipped through them. It was as big
as my mother's uncle Murray, and white,
with large brown counties on its body.

We held each other's gaze, its face
pushed up so close to me
if it has opened its snout
I'd have fallen in.

SUE CHENETTE

THE TRAIN ON ALL SAINTS DAY

If I could tell you
the name of every tree sprung up
along the rails – poplar
lime tree, chêne,
plane tree – enumerate
the globes of mistletoe,
feathered crowns against
blue scrimmed and streaked
with cloud and jet trails,
wash of sun, if

I could tell you exactly
the lean of trunks, angles
of branches, weight of the topmost
pine bough lopped over, or

the number of stones in that steeple
thinning into sky, slant of sunlight
falling on new green
winter wheat, on yellow chrysanthemums
in the walled cemetery, if I could

tell you the force
of current in the river,
the camber of the arc made
by the back of each
of three workers in the brown field,

the height this tower would reach
if its thrust were not
truncated, the dimensions
of aluminum slats in the siding
of this warehouse, vector of
light bounced from the small red car
passing on the highway, the density
of white mesh canopied over
espaliered apple trees, the overlap
of graffiti lettered on a station wall,
or the petals of a coral rose
caught in light, then

could you find me, triangulate
from these coordinates
my latitude, minutes, trajectory —
and could you tell me,
just where I am
along this mortal track
beneath a sweep of sky?

IMPRINT
(for Jory)

A bird hurtled onto the window this morning
like a catapulted boy
into a tree and
in that sliver-second I thought
the thwakk against the pane
was a gun blast
or
the pierce of telephone-speak
on my eardrum.

There was a perfect imprint on the glass:
      wing span spread like arms
      flung out to brake
            did the sunlight on the glass slant just-so?
      head twisted askew as if he noticed a
      last sliver-second navigation error
            did he see magnetic heaven on the other side?
      each feather clearly lined like fresh hairs
      sketched on a baby's scalp
            did the unforgiving tree feel the boy's branding?

A cartwheeled prayer flung on my
morning pane.

SUSAN GILLIS

GARBAGE

The dead can hear
wind as it riffles a pool of water after rain.
Birdsong through their barricaded doors.
They can hear
the shuffling feet and wailing praise of those who deliver
the golden goods into their tombs,
and the shuffling and grunts and curses
of those who deliver them of their worldly goods.
Every morning the trucks drive into our square
to deliver us from garbage with noisy salvation.
Your eyes open slowly while over your face the sun
waves its gold glove. The dead can hear
our heartbeats

and the shutting of an eye in an empty tomb.
At the moment of the rain's stopping,
of the first bud and the first
shoot of grass,
a bead of water falls

whether from a lintel or a bird's wing
or an eye

and the dead can hear it,
it falls onto their throats

and when it leaves, it leaves a thin rime.

SUE GOYETTE

IT'S NOT KEENING, IT IS A KIND OF HUNGER

I had swallowed a bird whole, that's what people thought. I tried telling them
that no, I hadn't swallowed a bird, I just didn't feel like talking

and the feathers coming out of my mouth were just a kind of silence, billowing.
When moths started coming out of my mouth, they thought I'd been a room

with a door closed for decades and now opening. In a way, they were right
but not about the door. I'm not a room, I wrote in a note I'd give

to whoever asked. My father has just died and the moths are the years
of silence between us finally taking wing. Yes, you could say an opening.

They'd step closer to me then, their hand reaching for my arm, my shoulder.
Oh, they'd say, your father. And he'd appear then, between us,

an urban river, smokestack or an eight lane expressway to cross. My father.
The clouds, the day he died, were sweaters draped over the shoulders

of the soft hills I looked to. The weather, maternal, tucking me in
and bringing me cool cloths for my forehead. I unfolded the chart

of the continent I'd just walked and was exhausted. All my clothes heaped
in the hamper, the animals set loose, the tinderbox dropped into the edge

of the Atlantic. This happens after a long journey, no? Every step you've taken,
every long shadow, each road appears briefly to bow before retiring.

Are you okay, people ask, and when I open my mouth an ocean pours out,
not a postcard ocean, but a real one, with cold-blooded creatures skulking

at the bottom, their hunger on a separate hunt moving farther from their mouths.

SUZANNE BOWNESS

TEN MINUTES AFTER THE BAD NEWS

She chose to see the birds as a sign.
That morning, they flew by her apartment window,
keen, a whisper, almost but not quite in formation.

Thrusting their white undersides towards her
they rush the building, gliding indifferently past.

She closed her eyes as if to feel their gust—
imaginary wind through her hair

(in spite of having chosen this corner apartment
deliberately for its double-paned glass; the only real sounds that day
were the urgent voices on CNN)

On other mornings when the birds had rushed by
she sometimes moved quickly to the other window—

it gave her a thrill to see their bodies re-emerge after the corner,
to witness how gracefully they banked the turn.

But this day she focussed instead
on the stillness in their wake,
and the skyline beyond.

Wanting to remember the particulars of this morning
the sky's waking grey,
the calm of the unsuspecting city.

SUSAN HOLBROOK

OOLICHAN BOOKS IS SEEKING SUBMISSIONS FOR A NEW ANTHOLOGY OF FEMALE CANADIAN POETS NAMED SUSAN

In 1942, a nice pregnant lady in Brantford thought Susan was a pretty name. By 1975 there were 37 million Susans in the English speaking world. Everywhere. Benign. Upholstery. Susans get it in on time. We are the kind of girl you marry. We are mistaken for Anne. We offer you almonds and dried apricots from our bag. We bought them at the Bulk Barn. You call our name constantly, but we stop turning our heads after a while. You meant another Susan. When we lose our temper we stomp our long but slender feet and you laugh. As kids the best you could come up with was Susan Bosom or pretending to call a pig. Aside from B. Anthony, we don't make waves. Get Gloria to raise the roof. Unglamourous, except for Susan Lucci. When you see Susan Lucci do you think Susan? No, you think Susan Lucci. Or Erica Kane. And nobody calls Susan Lucci Sue. Sure, we know that our name comes from the Hebrew Shoshana and means Graceful Lily, and variants include Sukie, Sosamma, and Zsa Zsa (we do our homework!) but it's no use because when a salesman wants to establish intimacy, he will call us Sue. We hate it but don't protest because that would suggest pretensions. If we were not Susans we would tear his ears off with our teeth. Actually some of us do go by Sue, but salesmen are afraid to establish intimacy with *us* and use Ma'am or, occasionally, Sir. Susans, lately I've noticed us in the bleachers, drinking tea from thermoses, wearing white baseball caps. We marvel at handheld devices, at the flying thumbs of people in their 30s. Stop it. Let's wear black baseball caps, strap on the Gatorade and do a triathlon or screw that and instead make out all day and have Fritos for dinner. Let's try road rage. Let's call someone the asshole that they are. Sue does it. Susans bristling, foaming, peeling up from the furniture. Dropping from the ceiling like Alabama cockroaches. If all the Susans turned off the nice. If all the Susans pulled at once. If your poems are accepted, we will require a proof of your name as Susan, or a reasonable variant, (e.g. photocopy of your driver's license

SUSAN McCASLIN

JUST AN ORDINARY WOMAN

One morning a white lamb
is placed in an ordinary woman's womb,

so petite, so delicate
no one notices.

So it might have been
with Mary,

sensing the black hooves
pricking the lining of her womb.

But I am no virgin.
Nevertheless, it is the creature's time,

who pushes against the walls
of a garden grown too small.

She slips out easily, the white one.
Still, the binding cord holds.

My scissors are blunted;
hands fall back on sheets.

The strand unravels of itself
and the lamb rolls over alive

her eyes hurtling into mine.
Sun licks her clean.

How will I protect
such a secret offspring?

SUSAN GILLIS

THE MARRIAGE BED

I won't say I didn't watch her leave.
Boots all the way to her knees.
Hair to her waist.
Striding between the tables
and the dim sum carts.
In her dark lips and
insouciance she looked
like your best friend's daughter.
That is, not yours but anyone's.
Your best friend's daughter,
and here I do mean yours,
has a gravelly voice, albeit musical,
the voice of a much older woman
that erupts from her as though
the woman of the future
exists inside her, impatient
for knowledge and form.
That girl was like that.
After she left the washroom, I went in.
Later at home I thought of her kiss
on the tissue on top of the pile in the bin,
black almost, under the halogen light.
How light deepens the darkness of dark.
The twinning rode with me all night.

DOG AND COMET, APRIL 13

The black dog beside me on the porch
fades in the darkness as storm cells
billow from the south, gnawing starlight.

I whisper Joey and her tail sweeps
like brushes on a snare drum — hush hush.
See — all the sky churns. The ancient comet

strikes at the horizon, the borealis
flickers, pale colour rush, mercury
tipped on a slate floor. Like the comet,

the stars should shift nightly, be ephemeral,
inconclusive. No use for navigating.
This valley is the world. I see the comet

fall into Hellroaring Creek. I brace myself
for impact, expect ice crystals to flay
my face in a moment of incapacitating light.

MISS-STEP

Morning light polishes the kitchen window.
The crows decimate your sunflowers
pulling and stabbing in frantic head bobs.
And on the shed wall, the Boston ivy blazes red
blood leaves dripping.

A flowered apron drapes your slender hips
tiny bluebells dance across the fabric.
You are frying perfect eggs.
For just this moment, the children like their breakfast.

What if the children disappear?

You are about to step onto the smooth wood
tilting inwards, a sudden long slide towards terror.
Your heart thumps its steady rhythm and then it is
clanging and clamouring in your chest, throbbing against your bones
a fist battering your ribcage.
Your breath squeezes down its narrow tunnels.
Cold sweat pools between your breasts.
Your skin squeezes tight against your ribs.
You can't breathe, the tiny hairs on your neck stand erect and quivering.

Or, maybe purple-bellied clouds rear up and the sky begins to twist.
Your laundry whips on the line, frantic bodies wanting to escape.
Danger drenches the day
hard rain driving at your face, tears blurring.
Your ragged breathing claws at your throat, seeking an escape.

Then, the sun slides from beneath the bruised clouds
and glances off your silver teapot.
The wind sighs, rippling the clothing on the line.
The children slip in the garden gate.
The perfect eggs sizzle and pop.

SUSAN CORMIER

letter from an editor: album version

April 2, 2008

dear mr rob mclennan;

on behalf of the *Rain City Review* magazine editorial board, I thank you for yr poetry submission dated May 15, 2000. the image of her sleeping, in the wrong city, while paint moved, or was moved by you. of five editors, four wrote <u>yes</u>, underlined. rare that we agree with such enthusiasm. rare that we agree. enthusiasm. we have

good intentions, better wine, are easily distracted by passersby. we fall in love randomly. we fall, love randomly, bewildered by our own awkwardness. perhaps you can relate.

since   , yr blue period poems have turned read, printpressed shelved sold. may I remind you that we do not publish previously. we do not publish. she still sleeps; the paint has long since dried. previously published, we do not. is paint like glass: slow liquid, falling.

yr selfaddressed stamped best laid plans. you apparently live in linear time. we live in East Vancouver. did you really think we would reply before postage went up. we count the days

of the month on our knuckles, stutter small paycheques. we sleep at odd hours, relish the slow stretch of bones in morning cold. we have crows, explosions of crows crowding the sky with wings. when wind picks up we leave the park with guitars & coffeecups, stand in doorways & watch clocks blow by. we have learned from leaving our notebooks in the rain. my home crowds

with drying paintings, crow feathers, notebooks that explode at opening doors. in my filing cabinet, yr poems unfolded flat, dead copy carefully kept for blueline editing on a print run that never pressed paper. in yr 2002 compilation, said poems appear on pages 88 through 90, or 86 through 88, depending on numbered pages or table of contents. I commend yr copyeditor on quiet confusioning. may I remind you, we do not publish previously. we intend to go to press immediately. we are

working on it: leaning into the rain or out of it, turning our shoulders towards or away from each other, gathering fallen notepaper from corners & alleys. a group of crows is an intrigue. dried paint falls slowly. we intend

to go to press immediately upon receipt of revenue for neversold advertising. since our last board meeting, our features editor has moved west, our president has lost 100 pounds, our newest member has left for Cuba, & our advertising director has passed away. when the

trees take the sunlight we drink wine & sit on patios, lean elbows into passerby conversation, talk about thin shadows & crows, who's gone wintermad in old rain. we slip & skid in grey snow slurry, hold our coats closed against wind or open against falling, fists twisting in pockets of holes & old notes crushed by fingertips. we are working on it. perhaps you can relate

to our silences, the past lovers we claim broke us, forgiveness of drunk friends' hands. you can relate,

perhaps. payment is in copies. they are in the mail, will arrive by morning. though whose morning. she sleeps

through the rain. paint has yet dried, is still falling. crows & notebook pages are blown off-course. perhaps she has left: in her dreams, in yours. we watch the crows, muse misremembered kisses, write on unlined paper, redefine linear. in lieu of

publication, please accept punctuation. please accept this beautiful breakdown of language, this noun without definition. a looseleafed book

blown on the lawn. wind, pages. a black wool coat snapped
open against falling,   /wings.

SUSAN PLETT

WHAT THE ADOPTION AGENCY DOESN'T SAY

she places the baby
in my arms, settles
the mantle of motherhood
on my shoulders

They tell us a story
we are eager to hear –
the desperate teenager with her
unplanned complication, an erratic
aberration in her carefree life
The birthmother. Birthfather.
Nine months is all they need,
all the time they want,
they're looking forward to the day
she places the baby

I am reluctant to think it's that easy,
that someone could give away
what I have spent these long years
aching for, the shadow of that tiny missing piece
darkening the sky on even the bluest of days.
Who are these people?
who can walk away
without a backward glance
at a milky blue-eyed bundle
settled in my arms?

They do not exist. Know this,
in your rocking chair at midnight,
your nose pressed – oh, at last! – against

a sleepy scented head - somewhere
a mother cries herself to sleep,
breasts hardened with un-needed milk.
Somewhere a grandmother tucks
a pair of booties into the back of a drawer.
Knit this into the fabric of
your mantle of motherhood.

And know this, when you dare:
You will lose count of the parents and grandparents.
And the child who reached up and pulled the sun
back into your sky will push out of your arms
and ask "Why wasn't I good enough to keep?"

Know this, in your rocking chair, in the early
days, and be sparing with the pretty words
you use to tell the story. There's a lot resting
on your shoulders.

SUE MACLEOD

TO A FRIEND WITH HER DAUGHTER, WASHING DISHES

We speak of old age, and put it away
again: thought on a string.
I sip your good, strong coffee
while we joke about our forties
as a dress rehearsal.
Curtain time ahead! We scare ourselves like kids
at movies. How we do
exaggerate, the way

I do now, convinced
that Lynne's movements are smoother,
more supple than yours
as you work together at the kitchen sink.
And when did her hair become thicker?
more auburn? I watch
her shoulder blades—a pair of wings
could sprout there. And she's the one
best able now to reach
the highest shelf.

There's a shift
taking place, this is just the beginning,
as if something's draining out of us
and into them. Remember how *big*
we were once? We were
giants of women.

With young daughters riding the curves
of our hips, we'd glide through our rooms
collecting *Mommy's keys*, and *Mommy's wallet*.

We were Olive Oyl.
We were Popeye, too.

                  ~⁄

A shaft of light
is falling through your window now
and spreads to every surface.
There are no clear
delineations, not
like in the swimming lessons
when the girls were small. The comfort
of badges, of lanes.
And no bigger miracles, maybe, than this:
that we're talking in the kitchen, still, and our girls
nearly grown. And there'll be no
well-marked corridor to old
from not old yet—only
gradations of light, of heat
touching and leaving
the skin.

But what do I know?
sitting here with my coffee
where I can still play
with an image like this one:
that we're all enrolled in the same
dusty classroom, an old-fashioned classroom,
early afternoon, lingering odour
of paperbag lunches
from home, and they're writing on the blackboard
with their backs to us, our large and shining
children, and the chalk they're using
used to be our bones.

SUE SINCLAIR

DELAY

Quarter of an hour, half an hour,
still no train. All of us thinking of home and how
we're not there and will or won't be missed,
how the surface of our life goes on elsewhere
even as we stand here, our absence
snail-paced, cumulative.

We settle in, inhabit ourselves uneasily,
make peace with our half-existence.
Then a dog starts to howl, and though no one
so much as flinches, something tightens
over the space between us.
Some abstract noun, larger and more meaningful
than we care to imagine, has pushed
its way in and is growing bigger by the second.

How could anything suffer so long, so hopelessly?
Yet the sound doesn't relent, and the faces
around me won't let it register,
won't so much as blink. I feel the indifference
on my own face and don't know who I am anymore:
I've fled, but how, and to where?

I picture it, despite myself: the platform ahead, the ambulance,
and the altered faces of those who couldn't stop
whoever it was. The howl becomes the sound
of the soul pushed to the edge of itself,
facing up to a world which it still, after all these years,
is not really convinced it must inhabit.

And because the crowd presses in on all sides
and I can't see and so can't even be sure
it's a dog, I'm frightened, thinking the sound could
in a way be me, a voice from the part of me
I've tried not to know.

SUE GOYETTE

FOR WOMEN WHO CRY WHEN THEY DRIVE

Blame it on the CBC stereo if anyone asks. Blame it on
the viola. I did and it worked. I never even had to mention locksmiths

and lovers, how close the two are. I never had to name
each white-knuckle grip of his on the steering wheel. I'll name it here, though,

for you. Surrender and all its aliases. I feel at home in two places now.
One's here, the other in the library surrounded by reference books

to the stars. Driving doesn't help. But you already know that. Remember
when you stopped, pulled over on Cole Harbour Road and wept,

bowed to the wheel and the long road ahead, the long road behind. I tried
signalling, pulling over, but the traffic was stubborn. If you are reading this,

I did try to stop. The passing lanes of loss and love and the speed limit
to this life. I held you for days in my heart, dear sad woman in the dark green Volvo

next to the Dairy Queen, next to the Royal Bank, feeling like you have no choice.
And you don't. You don't, except to fasten your seat belt

and yield.

SUSAN MUSGRAVE

ALL I WANTED WAS TO LIE

in bed with the black cat curled against
my spine, listening to the rain, the wind.
I didn't want to rise, dress, take a taxi
to another airport, my body refusing to switch
from Irish time no matter how often I face
myself in the mirror and say *wake up*
you are not in Donegal, you are not
in Sligo, you are no longer in Connemara.
All I wanted, - but then the cat brought a rat in
from the drowning rain – all I needed at three a.m.
Pacific Standard Time but, as far as my body
was concerned, 11 a.m. in Ballydown. I plucked
the luckless rat from the cat's paws
and dropped it in the compost bucket
full of old tea and swollen leaves, a happier
death, it seemed to me, but the shocked
rat revived: doesn't everything only want to live?
All I wanted was to return to my bed and spend
the rest of the night dreaming, but woke instead
screaming at Stephen because he was high
on pharmaceuticals. The sadness I feel these days
is no ordinary sadness; all I want is to lie down
with the sound of the rain on the roof
of my skull, the black cat beside me purring
its murderous self to sleep. But when I think
of Stephen giving up and going back to prison
even the rain is no consolation. I haven't felt
this much desolation since I left Ireland two days ago,
my mother in the aisle seat next to me

offering Mento after Mento, as if feeding my sadness
something sweet might pacify the grief.
You want sweet? I used to drive the frozen 401
from Kitchener to Kingston to visit Stephen at Millhaven
Penitentiary: how many times I rose from my bed at three a.m.,
dressed and drove through the dark because I loved him
and believed, back then, that love... I believed, back then...
I no longer know what I tried to believe. Now the black stone
of my heart is sinking under its own weight, worn out from living
in the wet collapse of the wound for so long even death
feels unreliable tonight, in the faithless rain and wind.

THE SUSAN/SUSIE/SUZANNAH/SUE/SUZANNES

SUSIE PETERSIEL BERG
Susie Petersiel Berg is a Toronto writer and editor. Her work has appeared in several journals, and she is the author of the chapbook, *Paper Cuts*. She is frequently featured on the poetry reading stages of Toronto.

SUZANNE BOWNESS
Suzanne (Sue) Bowness has been working as a freelance writer/editor for over ten years. In 2010, she published her first collection of poetry *The Days You've Spent* (Tightrope Books) and in 2006 she won the Ottawa Little Theatre's National One-Act Playwriting Competition. She is currently working on several other creative projects.

SUSAN BRALEY
Susan Braley lives in Victoria, BC. Her poetry has appeared in various publications, including *Walk Myself Home, Canadian Woman Studies, Island Writer*, and *Arc Poetry Magazine*. Her poem "Giving Him Up" placed first in the poetry category in the 2012 Victoria Writers' Society Annual Writing Contest; her poem "Traces" was shortlisted for *Arc*'s 2010 Poem of the Year and won the Readers' Choice Award.

SUSAN BRISCOE
Susan Briscoe has won the Lina Hartrand Award and has been shortlisted for the Gerald Lampert and CBC Literary Awards. She earned her MA in creative writing from Concordia University and currently teaches English at Dawson College in Montreal. "Saboteurs" is a combination of two separate, untitled poems from *The Crow's Vow*, published in 2010 by Vehicule Press (Signal Editions).

SIOUX BROWNING (BORN SUSAN)
Sioux was granted her first name in Grade 9 by a friend who was a fan of Siouxsie and the Banshees. The notion of writing for a living occurred to her late, after many, many random jobs: bottling spices, ski liftie, treeplanter, shipper of upholstery fabric... She has written for a number of Canadian TV shows, published poems and non-fiction pieces in periodicals and anthologies, and has taught screenwriting for seven years for UBC. She loves to write in several genres but only very, very slowly. She lives in BC with her Sweetpea and several quadrupeds.

SUSAN BUCHANAN
Lives in beautiful Prince Edward Island with her partner and two standard poodles. They have a lovely 21-year-old daughter. She has been writing all her life but only seriously for the last two years. She writes poetry and short stories and is at work on a novel.

SUE CHENETTE
Sue Chenette, a classical pianist as well as a poet, is the author of *The Bones of His Being* (Guernica Editions, 2012) and *Slender Human Weight* (Guernica Editions, 2009), as well as three chap-books: *Solitude in Cloud and Sun*, *A Transport of Grief*, and *The Time Between Us*, which won the Canadian Poetry Association's Shaunt Basmajian Award in 2001.

SUSAN CONSTABLE
Susan Constable's Japanese poetry forms have been published in over forty online and print journals in North America, Europe, Asia, and Australia. Her haiku and tanka continue to appear in numerous anthologies and have received considerable recognition in international contests. She lives with her husband in Nanoose Bay, BC. Her untitled poem previously appeared in 8th place, Best of Issue, *Presence*, #40, 2010.

SUSAN CORMIER
Susan "Queen of Crows" Cormier is a multimedia industrial poet. She has won or been shortlisted for awards including CBC's National Literary Award, Arc Magazine's Poem of the Year, and the Federation of B.C. Writers' Literary Writes.

SUSAN DRAIN
Susan Drain lives in Nova Scotia. In recent years she seems to have found the voice that was silenced by a life spent in academe. It has been a rich and satisfying life, but writing is better. And even harder.

SUSAN ELMSLIE
Susan Elmslie's *I, Nadja, and Other Poems*, won the A.M. Klein Poetry Prize and was shortlisted for the McAuslan First Book Prize, the Pat Lowther Award and a ReLit Award. Her poems also appear in several journals, anthologies, and in a prize-winning chapbook. Canada Council grants have supported her work.
"First Apology To My Daughter", "How the Litchi Came to Be", "Pisces You Swim in Two Directions", and "Lump" were published in her book, *I, Nadja, and Other Poems* (Brick, 2006). "Lump" was also published in *The Bright Well: Contemporary Canadian Poems about Facing Cancer*, edited by Fiona Tinwei Lam (Leaf Press, 2011).

SUSAN (CROWE) FENNER
Susan (Crowe) Fenner is a former drama and dance teacher. She analyzes her dreams, copilots a Cessna, and is founder of Grannies à Gogo in Vernon, BC. Her short fiction and non-fiction has been published in journals in Canada (*Descant, Existere, Maple Tree Supplement, Danforth Review*), the USA, England and South Africa.

SUE GEE

Sue Gee is a graduate of UVic's creative writing program. Her poems have been published in *Event*, *Prairie Fire* and The *Antigonish Review*, and she is currently working on her first manuscript. She lives in Victoria.

SUSAN GILLIS

Susan Gillis is a poet, teacher, and member of the poetry collective Yoko's Dogs. *Volta* (Signature, 2002) won the A. M. Klein Prize for Poetry. Her most recent books are *The Rapids* (forthcoming from Brick) and *Twenty Views of the Lachine Rapids* (Gaspereau, 2012). *Whisk*, in collaboration with Yoko's Dogs, will be published by Pedlar Press in 2013. Susan divides her time between Montreal and a rural hamlet near Perth, Ontario.

SUSAN GLICKMAN

Susan Glickman's sixth book of poetry, *The Smooth Yarrow*, came out in 2012 as did her second novel, *The Tale-Teller*. Her first novel, *The Violin Lover* (2006), won the Canadian Jewish Fiction Award. She is also the author of the "Lunch Bunch" series of children's books and of *The Picturesque & the Sublime* (1998). "Running in Prospect Cemetery" first came out in *Running in Prospect Cemetery: New & Selected Poems* (Montréal: Signal Editions, 2004); "After Pasternak" in *Complicity* (Montréal: Signal Editions, 1983); "Poem about your laugh" in *Henry Moore's Sheep and Other Poems* (Montréal: Signal Editions 1990). "On Finding a Copy of Pigeon in the Hospital Bookstore" appeared in the *2011 Global Poetry Anthology* and *The Smooth Yarrow*, (Signal Editions).

SUE GOYETTE

Sue Goyette lives in Halifax, Nova Scotia and has published three books of poems, *The True Names of Birds, Undone, and outskirts* (Brick Books) and a novel, *Lures* (HarperCollins, 2002). Her fourth collection of poems, *Ocean*, is forthcoming from Gaspereau Press in 2013. "For Women Who Cry When They Drive" and "Alone" were first published in *Undone* (Brick Books, 2004), "It's not keening, it is a kind of hunger" was published in *The True Names of Birds* (Brick Books, 1998) and "A Collage of Seasons for a Grieving Widow" was published in *outskirts* (Brick Books, 2011).

SUSAN ANDREWS GRACE

Selections from "Hypatia's Wake" appeared in *Rocksalt: An Anthology of Contemporary BC Poetry*, 2007 (eds Mona Fertig and Harold Rhenisch) and is forthcoming in *CV2*. Susan Andrews Grace lives in Nelson, BC where she also maintains a visual art practice.

SUSAN HALDANE

When Susan Haldane was born, her parents briefly considered naming her Shoshana. Now she lives in a many-Susan community in northern Ontario, where she and her husband and two sons operate a farm. Her work has previously been published in *Room* and *The New Quarterly*.

Susan Holbrook

Susan Holbrook is the author of the Trillium-nominated *Joy Is So Exhausting* (Coach House, 2009) and *misled* (Red Deer 1999), which was shortlisted for the Pat Lowther Memorial award and the Stephan G. Stephansson award. She recently co-edited *The Letters of Gertrude Stein and Virgil Thomson: Composition as Conversation* (Oxford UP, 2010). She teaches at the University of Windsor with a number of other Susans. "Good Egg Bad Seed" first appeared as a chapbook (Nomados, 2004), and then also appeared in *Joy Is So Exhausting* (Coach House, 2009).

Susan Ioannou

Susan Ioannou is a Toronto poet, who also writes literary essays and fiction. Recent poetry books include *Coming Home: An Old Love Story* (Leaf Press) and *Looking Through Stone: Poems about the Earth* (Your Scrivener Press); also the guide *A Magical Clockwork: The Art of Writing the Poem* (Wordwrights Canada). "Balkan Winter" was first published in *Where the Light Waits*, (Victoria: Ekstasis Editions, 1996) and Subsequently in *Ygdrasil*, December 2003. "Srebrenica Suite" was first published in *Vintage 1994* (Toronto: The League of Canadian Poets, 1995), and in *Where the Light Waits* (Victoria: Ekstasis Editions, 1996). "The Comfort of Elders" was first published in *Canadian Literature*, No. 149, Summer 1996.

Sue Kanhai

Sue Kanhai is a Toronto-based writer whose work has appeared in newspapers, magazines, books, and online. She holds a degree in French language, literature, and translation from the University of Toronto and is currently completing a certificate in creative writing from U of T's School of Continuing Studies.

Sue MacLeod

Sue MacLeod lives in Toronto, works as a freelance editor and is on the verge of completing a new poetry manuscript. Her young adult novel, *Namesake*, will be published in 2013. Sue's poetry collections are *That Singing You Hear at the Edges* (Signature Editions) and *The Language of Rain* (Roseway). "No One Like Us", "This is a poem where words are the underpaid workers", and "To a friend with her daughter, washing dishes" were first published in *That Singing You Hear at the Edges* (Signature Editions).

Suzette Mayr

Suzette Mayr is the author of four novels and two poetry chapbooks, *If Adultery* and *Zebra Talk*. Her work has been nominated for several awards including the Giller Prize and a Commonwealth Regional Prize. She lives in Calgary.

Susan McCaslin

Susan McCaslin recent book of poetry, *Demeter Goes Skydiving* (University of Alberta Press, 2011) was a finalist for the BC Book Prize (Dorothy Livesay Award, 2012) and the winner of the Alberta Book Publishing Award (Robert Kroetsch Poetry Book Award, 2012). Susan recently published a volume of essays, *Arousing the Spirit* (Wood Lake Books, 2011).

Susan McMaster

Susan McMaster is past president of the League of Canadian Poets and author or editor of some 20 poetry collections and recordings. She has performed widely with First Draft, SugarBeat and Geode Music & Poetry; was founding editor of *Branching Out*, Canada's first national feminist magazine; and has led such projects as Convergence: Poems for Peace. "Lately, she remembers" and "2" are both from *Paper Affair: Poems Selected & New* (Black Moss Press, 2010).

Susan Musgrave

Susan Musgrave changes the spelling of her given name to Sioux-Zen, whenever she tires of being Only One of Many. Her most recent poetry collection is *Origami Dove*; a new novel, *Given*, will be published in the fall of 2012. She lives on Haida Gwaii and teaches poetry at UBC's Optional Residency MFA. "The Coroner at the Taverna", "All the Wild Winds" and "Mother's Day Behind the West Hotel" were published in *Origami Dove* (M&S, 2011); "You Didn't Fit" in *What the Small Day Cannot Hold: Collected Poems 1970-1985* (BeachHolme).

Susan Olding

Susan Olding's *Pathologies: A Life in Essays* won the Creative Nonfiction Collective's Readers' Choice Award for 2010. Her poetry and prose have appeared widely in magazines such as *CV2*, *Event*, the *L.A. Review of Books*, the *New Quarterly*, and the *Utne Reader*. She lives with her family in Kingston.

Susan Paddon

Susan Paddon lives and works on Cape Breton Island. She is currently working on a long poem series.

Susan Plett

Susan Plett writes poetry and prose from the home in Calgary, Alberta that she shares with one small dog, two engaging teenagers, and the most steadfast husband in the universe. Her work has appeared both online and in various print publications.

Suzanne Robertson

Suzanne Robertson is a writer and photographer living in Toronto. She works at the Children's Aid Society. Her first collection of poetry, *Paramita, Little Black* was nominated for the Gerald Lampert Award. It was published by Guernica Editions in 2011.

Suzannah Showler

Suzannah Showler holds an M.A. in Creative Writing from the University of Toronto. Her writing has appeared in various Canadian magazines. She collects narratives about lost objects on the blog Art of Losing.

SUSAN SIDDELEY

Susan Siddeley was born in Yorkshire, England, attended University in Wales and emigrated to Canada with her geologist husband in 1968. Nowadays, she divides her time between Toronto and Santiago, Chile, where her husband still works, and where they host annual writing retreats. She shops at No Frills, loves family teas, The Andes and maple donuts, and has recently launched a creative memoir, "Home First".

SUE SINCLAIR

Sue Sinclair has published four collections of poems, all of which have been nominated for national and regional awards. Her latest collection, *Breaker*, was published by Brick Books in 2008. Sue has been mistaken for other Canadian Sue-poets on more than one occasion, which she takes as a compliment. "Winter in the Garden" was published in *The Fiddlehead*, Summer 2010. "Control", "Claimed", "Devotion" and "Delay" were all published in *Breaker* (Brick Books, 2008).

SUE SORENSEN

Sue Sorensen lives in Winnipeg, where she teaches English at Canadian Mennonite University. She is author of the novel *A Large Harmonium* (winner of Best First Book at the Manitoba Book Awards and finalist in Winnipeg's On the Same Page for 2012) and editor of *West of Eden: Essays on Canadian Prairie Literature*.

SUZANNE M. STEELE

Suzanne M. Steele is the first poet to accompany Canadian troops into war as an official war artist. Her *Afghanistan: Requiem for a Generation*, the largest orchestral commission in Canadian history, premieres November 2012. Awarded an international scholarship to write her PhD, she resides in the U.K. with her daughter. "9 liner" was previously published in *In Arms: Soldier's Words*, published by the Edmonton Poetry Festival.

SUSAN STENSON

Susan Stenson is a poet living in Victoria where she works as a teacher and bodytalk practitioner. Since 1992, she's been co-publishing *The Claremont Review*, Canada's thriving literary magazine of teen poetry, art and fiction. She is married to the fiction writer, Bill Stenson. "The Crazy Maps" won the *Arc* Poetry Prize in 2004 and was also published in *My Mother Agrees with the Dead*, (Wolsak and Wyn, 2007). "Reader Response Theory" won *sub-Terrain*'s Great Literary Hunt Prize in 2004 and was published in *Nobody Move* (Sono Nis Press, 2010).

SUSAN STEUDEL

Susan Steudel is the author of *New Theatre* (Coach House Books, 2012). She lives in Vancouver where she belongs to a local writing collective and works as a court reporter.

SUSAN TELFER

Susan Telfer's first book was *House Beneath* (Hagios, 2009). Her poetry has been published in journals across Canada; she received the Gillian Lowndes Award in 2008. She lives in Gibsons, B.C. with her family, where she directs the Gibson's Live Poets Society. "Portrait" appeared in *Event*, Summer 2011

SUE WHEELER

Sue Wheeler has published three collections of poetry, from Kalamalka Press and Brick Books. She lives and works on a seaside farm on Lasqueti Island, BC. "Cold Hands" was published in *Slow-Moving Target,* (Brick Books, 2000) and "Understory" was published in *Habitat,* (Brick Books, 2005).

SUSAN YOUNG

Susan Young's poems have been published in many Canadian journals including *The New Quarterly* and *Poetry Canada*. Her manuscript "In the room that became a forest" received an Honourable Mention in the 2009 Alfred Bailey Poetry contest. A Vancouverite, Susan is currently working on her MFA through UBC's optional-residence program.

INDEX OF SUSANS

Sarah Yi-Mei Tsiang is the author of *Sweet Devilry* (Oolichan Books 2011), which won the Gerald Lampert prize in 2012. She is also the author of several children's books, including *A Flock of Shoes*, and *The Stone Hatchlings*, with Annick Press. Sarah's work has been published and translated internationally, and she considers herself one of the foremost experts on contemporary Canadian poets named Susan.